ANXIOUS ATTACHMENT RECOVERY SOLUTION

PRACTICAL TRANSFORMATIVE GUIDE TO OVERCOME FEAR OF ABANDONMENT, IMPROVE EMOTIONAL STABILITY, BOOST SELF-ESTEEM, AND BUILD SECURE LASTING RELATIONSHIPS

LUZIVETTE MARTINEZ, RN BSN

CONTENTS

INTRODUCTION

Have you ever wondered why certain relationships make you feel like you're on an emotional rollercoaster while others are stable and nurturing? This question isn't just philosophical—it's deeply personal and rooted in the science of attachment. My journey into the heart of attachment theory began over thirty years ago on the bustling floors of hospitals where emotional and psychological patterns often spelled the difference between healing and suffering.

Drawing on my extensive background as a registered nurse with a focus on psychological wellness, I have seen the profound disruption that an anxious attachment style can cause in both personal relationships and individual health. My professional experience, enriched by my own journey to decode these complex emotional patterns, has equipped me with valuable insights and strategies that I am excited to pass on to you.

The Anxious Attachment Recovery Solution is more than just a book; it's a practical, transformative guide designed to help you navigate the complexities of anxious attachment. Whether you're struggling to understand why you react a certain way in relationships or looking to foster deeper connections, this book is crafted for you. It combines professional expertise with heartfelt insights and real-life stories, offering a unique and powerful approach to overcoming the challenges of anxious attachment.

The prevalence of anxious attachment styles is more common than many might think, affecting a substantial portion of the population. These styles can lead to a persistent fear of abandonment and a plethora of relationship anxieties. However, the impact of these patterns can be mitigated, and the path to secure, fulfilling relationships is within your reach.

In the following pages, you will discover a transformative journey outlined through easy-to-follow practical steps. Each step is supported by theory, hands-on exercises, and narratives from real people who have walked this path. These stories are not just testimonials but mirrors reflecting the potential for change and growth.

As we explore these steps together, remember that healing is possible and within your grasp. This book is a tool to help you unlock a more secure and satisfying future in your relationships. With courage and hope, let's step forward together toward a life where your relationships are defined not by fear but by connection and security.

Welcome to a new beginning. Let this be the moment you start to rewrite your story.

1

UNDERSTANDING ANXIOUS ATTACHMENT

How often have you found yourself in a situation where a simple, unreturned phone call spiraled into a vortex of worry and assumptions that something was amiss in your relationship? This scenario, though seemingly insignificant, is a palpable illustration of the everyday struggles faced by those with an anxious attachment style. This chapter digs deep into the emotional tapestry of anxious attachment, unraveling the threads that compose its complex nature. With over three decades of experience in the realms of emotional and psychological wellness, I have observed the profound impact that attachment styles have on interpersonal relationships and individual peace of mind. Here, we will explore the symptoms and reactions associated with anxious attachment and the subtle ways it influences various aspects of life, including non-romantic relationships and professional environments. By understanding these dynamics, you are better equipped to navigate and reshape your relational world.

DECODING ANXIOUS ATTACHMENT: SIGNS AND SYMPTOMS

Identify Common Symptoms

Anxious attachment manifests through a spectrum of emotional and behavioral signs that often disrupt normal relationship dynamics. One of the most telling signs is the constant need for reassurance from partners or friends. This might look like frequent calls or texts seeking confirmation of the other person's feelings or intentions. Consider the case where you might send multiple messages to your partner throughout the day, not merely to share information but to quell an underlying fear of abandonment or disinterest. Similarly, difficulty enjoying time alone is another significant indicator. Individuals might feel restless or anxious when not accompanied by others, interpreting solitude as unwanted isolation rather than peaceful alone time.

Explore Emotional Responses

The emotional responses triggered by perceived threats in relationships can be intense and overwhelming for someone with an anxious attachment style. Anxiety spikes are common reactions to situations where these individuals feel their relational security might be threatened. For instance, a partner's delayed response to a text message might be interpreted not as a mere oversight but as a sign of waning interest or affection. This often leads to compulsive caregiving behaviors where the individual goes to great lengths to please or appease their partner, driven by an underlying fear that not doing so could result in rejection or abandonment.

Discuss Relationship Patterns

The relationship dynamics typical of anxious attachment often involve a misinterpretation of neutral actions as negative. For example, if a partner chooses to spend an evening with friends, the individual with anxious attachment might interpret this as a sign of relational drift rather than a healthy social interaction. This misinterpretation can lead to clinginess, where the person feels compelled to restore closeness to dispel their insecurities. This pattern strains relationships and places an undue emotional burden on the individual, who remains in a constant state of alert to any signs of perceived detachment.

Highlight Social Implications

Beyond romantic relationships, anxious attachment can significantly impact social interactions and professional life. Individuals may struggle with forming non-romantic relationships due to similar fears of abandonment or rejection from friends and colleagues. In the workplace, this attachment style might manifest as hypersensitivity to feedback or an excessive need for validation from peers or superiors, which can hinder professional growth and interpersonal relations. Understanding these broader implications is crucial, as they often reinforce the attachment style, perpetuating a cycle that might seem inescapable.

In the following sections, we will continue to explore the underlying psychological frameworks and developmental influences that contribute to the formation of anxious attachment. By delving into these areas, we aim to provide a more straight forward pathway toward understanding and addressing the roots and ramifications of this complex attachment style.

THE PSYCHOLOGY BEHIND ANXIOUS ATTACHMENT: WHAT THE RESEARCH SAYS

The fabric of our emotional lives is often woven from the threads of our earliest relationships, and is a concept profoundly articulated in the seminal works of John Bowlby, the father of attachment theory. Bowlby posited that the bonds formed between infants and their primary caregivers have lasting psychological implications, shaping how individuals perceive and interact in relationships throughout their lives. This theory laid the groundwork for understanding various attachment styles, including anxious attachment, characterized by a persistent fear of abandonment and an excessive need for relational security. Expanding on Bowlby's theory, Mary Ainsworth's research introduced the concept of attachment styles through her Strange Situation assessments, categorizing them into secure, avoidant, and anxious. Anxiously attached individuals often find themselves in a relentless pursuit of closeness to their partners, driven by an underlying fear that they might be left alone without constant validation.

Recent studies have delved deeper into the nuances of how these attachment styles manifest in the brain's architecture and function. Neuroimaging research has shown that individuals with an anxious attachment style may have heightened activity in parts of the brain associated with emotional processing and anxiety, such as the amygdala. These findings suggest that their experiences of relationships are not only psychologically distressing but are also deeply rooted in neurobiological processes. This heightened sensitivity to relational cues often leads to a hyper-vigilant state, where even minor signs of disinterest from a partner can trigger profound anxiety and compulsive caregiving behaviors.

The interplay between anxious attachment and mental health cannot be overstated. Statistical data reveals a striking correlation between anxious attachment and a higher prevalence of mental health disorders, such as anxiety and depression. This relationship is likely bidirectional, where the chronic stress and emotional turmoil associated with anxious attachment exacerbate symptoms of mental health issues, which in turn can intensify feelings of insecurity and fear within relationships. Understanding this interconnection provides a crucial perspective for addressing not only the symptoms but also the root causes of emotional distress in anxiously attached individuals.

Despite these challenges, the research also brings a message of hope and transformation. Studies in psychology and neuroscience underscore the brain's remarkable plasticity, suggesting that it can reshape one's attachment style with appropriate therapeutic interventions and personal effort. Therapeutic approaches such as cognitive-behavioral therapy (CBT) and dialectical-behavior therapy (DBT) are effective in helping individuals understand and manage their anxiety, develop healthier ways of relating to others, and gradually build a sense of security in relationships. This potential for change is not merely theoretical. Still, it is supported by numerous case studies and clinical experiences that highlight the capacity for individuals to move towards more secure attachment patterns, thereby enhancing their relational and personal well-being.

Incorporating these insights into daily life and therapeutic practices offers a beacon of hope for those caught in the throes of anxious attachment. By grounding our understanding of attachment in robust research and embracing the possibility of change, we open the door to more fulfilling and emotionally healthy lives.

HOW EARLY EXPERIENCES SHAPE ATTACHMENT STYLES

The imprints of our early experiences are like subtle yet persistent whispers shaping how we interact with the world, particularly in our intimate relationships. From the moment we enter the world, the nature of the care we receive starts to mold our expectations and beliefs about ourselves and others. For those grappling with anxious attachment, understanding the influence of these early experiences is crucial in navigating a path toward healing and secure relationships.

Examine Childhood Influences

The role of parenting styles and early childhood interactions in shaping attachment styles cannot be overstated. Consider the scenario in which a child consistently experiences caregivers as intermittently available or emotionally unresponsive. Such children are likely to develop an anxious attachment style characterized by a pervasive fear that significant others will not be reliably responsive to their needs. Case studies in attachment research highlight that children who frequently encounter parental inconsistency tend to remain in a heightened state of alert, unsure when or if their emotional and physical needs will be met. This lack of predictability fosters an ongoing insecurity that can extend into adult relationships, manifesting as an incessant need for reassurance from partners or friends.

Discuss the Role of Trauma

Traumatic experiences such as loss, neglect, or emotional abuse during these formative years intensify the development of anxious attachment. Trauma disrupts a child's developing sense of safety and trust in the world. For instance, the loss of a parent or guardian can create a significant emotional void and a subsequent scramble for security. Neglect, whether emotional or physical, sends a potent message to the child that their needs are unimportant or unworthy of attention. This can translate into adulthood as a continual quest for validation and affection, often harming the individual's self-esteem and autonomy. These experiences embed a deep-seated fear of abandonment and an expectation that others will not provide the necessary emotional support, thereby setting a precedent for future relationships.

Explore the Impact of Positive Interactions

Contrasting these negative experiences, positive interactions during childhood, such as consistent nurturing and attuned caregiving, lay the groundwork for secure attachment. When caregivers are responsive to a child's needs, the child learns that they are worthy of love and that others can be trusted to provide support. This secure base allows the child to confidently explore the world and develop healthy, autonomous relationships in adulthood. The presence of a supportive caregiver teaches resilience and fosters a sense of stability that can buffer against the development of anxiety in relationships.

Introduce Resilience Factors

Despite adverse early experiences, certain factors can mitigate their long-term effects, fostering resilience and promoting healthier attachment styles. The presence of at least one consistent, supportive adult in a child's life can be a significant protective factor. This person could be a relative, teacher, or family friend who provides the child with a reliable source of emotional comfort and stability. Engagement in community activities such as sports, the arts, or youth groups offers a sense of belonging and opportunities for developing interpersonal skills and self-efficacy. These experiences can counterbalance the effects of earlier adverse experiences, providing alternative narratives and models for relationships that emphasize trust, cooperation, and mutual respect.

Understanding these foundational influences is a vital step in addressing the roots of anxious attachment. By exploring the contours of our earliest relationships, we uncover the origins of our relational dynamics and begin to see the possibility for change. This knowledge empowers individuals to reframe their narratives and actively seek healing and growth within their current and future relationships, ultimately leading to a life characterized by deeper connections and emotional security.

THE ROLE OF GENETICS AND ENVIRONMENT IN ATTACHMENT FORMATION

The intricate dance between our genetic makeup and the environments we navigate shapes much of who we are, including how we connect and bond with others. While exploring attachment styles often focuses on psychological and social factors, burgeoning research into genetic predispositions and epigenetics provides a fascinating layer to our understanding of human relationships. It's crucial to recognize that while our genetic makeup may lay the groundwork for certain predispositions toward attachment styles, the interplay with our environmental experiences truly shape these patterns. This holistic view highlights the complex intertwining of nature and nurture in our developmental outcomes.

Discuss Genetic Predispositions

Research in the realm of behavioral genetics suggests that our genes may indeed influence certain aspects of our attachment styles. Studies involving twins, for instance, have shown a moderate genetic component to how secure or anxious individuals feel in relationships. These findings might suggest that some of us could be more predisposed to developing anxious attachment styles than others. However, it is critical to underscore that these genetic factors do not act as direct scripts dictating our relational fates. Instead, they are better understood as inclinations that may make us more susceptible to certain feelings or behaviors, which can be mitigated or exacerbated by our life experiences. For example, a genetic tendency towards heightened sensitivity to stress could contribute to an anxious attachment if an individual is exposed to inconsistent caregiving but could be less impactful in a supportive, stable relational environment.

Analyze Environmental Factors

The environment plays a paramount role in shaping attachment styles, often moderating or amplifying the influences of our genetic predispositions. From the quality of parental care to broader cultural contexts, these environmental factors weave through the fabric of our early experiences, sculpting our expectations and strategies for connecting with others. Family dynamics, such as the emotional availability of caregivers, set early examples and standards for what relationships look like. Similarly, cultural norms and values can influence attachment styles by prescribing how much emotional closeness or independence is appropriate in relationships. For instance, cultures that emphasize individual autonomy might foster more avoidant attachment styles, while those that value close familial bonds might incline towards more anxious or secure attachments. Understanding these environmental impacts allows us to see how similar genetic predispositions can lead to different attachment outcomes depending on the social and familial context in which a person develops.

Highlight Epigenetics

Epigenetics, the study of how our behaviors and environment can cause changes that affect how our genes work, extends our understanding of how attachment styles can be influenced across the lifespan. Unlike genetic changes, epigenetic modifications do not alter the DNA sequence but affect how cells read genes, turning some genes on or off. These changes can be triggered by experiences such as stress, diet, or exposure to toxins, but fascinatingly, they can also arise from interpersonal experiences and relationships. For example, a caregiver's consistent warmth and responsiveness can promote epigenetic changes that enhance the expression of genes involved in stress regulation, potentially offsetting genetic predispositions toward anxiety. This dynamic interplay underscores how our relationships and environments shape our psychological patterns and influence our biological processes, contributing to the malleability of our attachment styles.

Provide Holistic Views

Embracing a holistic perspective is essential when considering attachment styles' formation and potential evolution. By acknowledging genetics and the environment's roles, we equip ourselves with a more nuanced appreciation of the complexities involved. This understanding fosters compassion for ourselves and others, as it highlights the myriad factors that influence our ways of relating beyond our immediate control. Moreover, it empowers us to know that change is possible—that we can influence our genetic expressions and attachment styles by altering our environments, relationships, and responses. Whether through therapeutic interventions, supportive relationships, or personal development efforts, we have the capacity to reshape our attachment patterns in ways that foster more secure and fulfilling connections.

COMPARING ATTACHMENT STYLES: ANXIOUS, AVOIDANT, AND SECURE

Understanding the spectrum of attachment styles—Anxious, Avoidant, and Secure—offers a comprehensive framework for recognizing your patterns and how you may interact with others whose attachment styles differ from yours. Each style encapsulates distinct traits and behaviors that profoundly influence interpersonal relationships.

Anxious attachment, as explored, is characterized by a pervasive fear of abandonment and an overarching need for closeness and reassurance. Individuals with this style often find themselves in a persistent state of emotional tumult, particularly in their intimate relationships, where they crave constant validation from their partners. Avoidant attachment, on the other hand, stands almost in contrast. Here, individuals prize independence above closeness, often perceiving emotional intimacy as threatening their autonomy. They typically maintain emotional distance from their partners and withdraw at the hint of closeness or deeper emotional demands. Secure attachment is the balance between these extremes. Individuals with a secure style are comfortable with closeness and can maintain their independence without feeling threatened. They tend to have healthy, trusting relationships where communication is open and emotional needs are met with understanding and responsiveness.

The dynamics between these relationship styles can be complex, particularly between those with anxious and avoidant attachments. Often, these attachments create a push-pull dynamic that can be frustrating for both parties. For instance, the more an anxiously attached individual presses for closeness, the more an avoidant attached partner may withdraw, exacerbating the fears and insecurities of the anxious partner, which in turn, pushes them to cling tighter. This cycle, commonly known as the "anxious-avoidant trap," can be challenging to escape without awareness and effort from both sides.

Each attachment style brings its own set of challenges and strengths to relationships. While often perceived as overly needy or clingy, anxiously attached individuals also bring a high degree of sensitivity and attentiveness to relationships, qualities that can foster deep connections and empathy. Avoidant attached individuals, though often seen as distant, provide independence and self-sufficiency that stabilizes a partnership. Securely attached individuals, equipped to navigate closeness and independence adeptly, often find themselves in balanced and resilient relationships, capable of withstanding life's inherent stresses more effectively than other attachment styles.

Importantly, attachment styles are not static; they can evolve through experiences and relationships. This fluidity means that someone with an anxious or avoidant style has the potential to move towards a more secure attachment through personal development, therapy, and healthy relationships. Understanding that these styles are adaptable rather than fixed can be profoundly empowering. For instance, an anxiously attached individual can learn to cultivate self-reassurance and independence, reducing their reliance on external validation. Conversely, an avoidant individual can gradually learn to embrace intimacy, recognizing that closeness does not necessarily equate to losing freedom. Through such shifts, the landscape of one's relationships can profoundly change, leading to healthier and more fulfilling interactions.

Recognizing your attachment style and understanding how it interacts with others can illuminate the paths to healthier relationships and personal growth. The insights derived from understanding these attachment styles are invaluable, whether it is adjusting behaviors, enhancing communication, or reshaping one's approach to intimacy. They foster self-awareness and enhance our capacity to engage more constructively and compassionately with those around us. As we navigate these styles, we learn to adjust and thrive in our relationships, continually evolving toward security and mutual satisfaction.

SELF-ASSESSMENT: IDENTIFYING YOUR ATTACHMENT STYLE

One of the most enlightening steps in pursuing emotional growth and understanding is to identify your attachment style. This process illuminates your relationship patterns and sets a foundation for the transformative experiences that lie ahead. To assist you in this endeavor, I offer various assessment tools designed to gently guide you toward a more profound understanding of yourself. These tools include carefully crafted questionnaires and reflective exercises that are both introspective and revealing.

The questionnaires are structured to prompt recognition of behaviors and reactions you typically exhibit in relational contexts. For instance, you might encounter questions about how you respond to conflict, express affection, or deal with separation from loved ones. Each response will contribute to a profile that mirrors your predominant attachment style—anxious, avoidant, or secure. It's important to approach these questionnaires with an open heart and an honest mindset, as the accuracy of your answers significantly influences the clarity of the insights you gain.

Once you have completed these assessments, interpreting your results becomes the next crucial step. This isn't about labeling yourself but understanding the tendencies that often steer your interactions. If your results lean towards an anxious attachment style, you may recognize patterns of needing frequent reassurance in relationships or feeling preoccupied with your partner's availability. On the other hand, an avoidant attachment style might resonate with you if you prefer emotional distance and value independence over intimacy. Secure attachment will likely reflect a balanced approach where comfort with closeness and autonomy coexist harmoniously. Each style carries nuances, and understanding these can profoundly affect how you perceive and manage your relationships.

Reflecting on your personal history plays an instrumental role in this self-assessment process. This reflection involves reviewing your childhood experiences, relationships with parents or primary caregivers, and early social interactions. Consider moments that might have significantly impacted your perception of trust and safety. Perhaps a pivotal incident taught you to guard your emotions, or you experienced consistent support that made it easy to trust others. These reflections are not about dwelling in the past but connecting the dots that have led to your current attachment style. This understanding can be profoundly empowering, as it allows you to identify specific areas for growth and healing.

This self-assessment merely begins a deeper exploration into your relational dynamics and internal landscape. It sets the stage for the subsequent chapters, where we will delve into strategies and practices to help you reshape your attachment style, fostering healthier and more fulfilling relationships. The goal here is not to change who you are but to enhance your understanding of yourself and improve your interactions with others. Through this process, you open doors to new possibilities in your relationships and take significant steps toward emotional well-being.

As you continue to explore and apply the insights from your self-assessment, remember that this is a process of discovery and transformation. Each step you take moves towards a deeper connection with yourself and others, paving the way for lasting change and personal growth.

2

UNVEILING THE INNER CHILD

I magine for a moment that within each of us, lives a younger version of ourselves. This is not just a whimsical child of memory but an active, influential presence that shapes how we think, feel, and relate to others daily. This is your "inner child," a psychological concept representing the original nucleus of your personality and emotional life formed in your earliest years. For those grappling with anxious attachment, this inner child often bears silent witness to fears and needs that have not been fully addressed. Understanding and connecting with this part of yourself is not merely an exercise in self-awareness—it's a powerful step towards healing and emotional freedom.

MEET YOUR INNER CHILD: UNDERSTANDING ITS INFLUENCE

Identify the Inner Child Concept

The "inner child" encapsulates the emotions, experiences, and inno-cence of our earliest years. Psychologists assert that this aspect of our psyche retains the feelings and memories of those years and profoundly influences our current behavior and emotional well-being. For many, recognizing this internal presence is the first step in reconciling past traumas with their present life. It's about acknowledging that many of the fears and insecurities that we encounter have deep roots that stretch back to our formative years. Understanding this can be profoundly liberating, as it allows us to frame our emotional responses as something that can be understood, managed, and healed.

Link to Anxious Attachment

For those with anxious attachment styles, the inner child often remains in a state of hidden alertness, shaped by early experiences where emotional needs were not consistently met. This child within might still be seeking the security and assurance they missed during those crucial years. This can manifest as a heightened sensitivity to relational dynamics in adult relationships, where even minor disconnections or perceived signs of rejection can trigger deep-seated fears and insecurities. Recognizing that these intense reactions might echo unmet childhood needs can be a game-changer. It allows you to begin addressing these fears at their origin, providing comfort and assurance to your inner child that you are now capable of providing the security they once lacked.

Recognize Signs of an Active Inner Child

Identifying the behaviors and emotions that signal the influence of your inner child can be enlightening. Perhaps you find yourself inexplicably upset when a friend is late to meet you, or maybe you feel irrationally jealous when your partner spends time with others. These reactions often stem from the fears and needs of your inner child. By recognizing these signs, you can start to understand and soothe these deep-seated parts of yourself in real time. This awareness is crucial because it shifts your perception of your reactions from being irrational to understandable responses based on past experiences.

Illustrate through Examples

Consider the story of Anna, a 35-year-old software developer who found herself constantly anxious about her relationships. Through therapy, she discovered that her fears of abandonment were echoes of the emotional neglect she experienced as a child. Her inner child was still seeking validation and security that she didn't receive consistently growing up. By recognizing this, Anna began to work on reassuring her inner child, addressing her anxiety from the root rather than just managing its symptoms. She started to implement routines that reinforced her sense of security and self-worth—practices like affirmations, self-soothing techniques, and setting healthy boundaries in her relationships. Over time, Anna reported feeling more stable in her relationships and less governed by her fears. Her story is a testament to the healing that becomes possible when we connect with and reassure our inner child.

THE LINK BETWEEN INNER CHILD WOUNDS AND ADULT RELATIONSHIPS

In the tapestry of our emotional lives, threads from our childhood experiences weave persistently through the fabric of our adult relationships. Particularly for those who bear the scars of emotional neglect or abuse from their early years, these threads can color interactions with a deep hue of anxious attachment. Imagine carrying a backpack from your past that you cannot set down; this is akin to moving through life with unresolved inner child wounds. These wounds frequently manifest in adult relationships as patterns of behavior that emerge from our deepest vulnerabilities—often without our conscious awareness. When these patterns are activated, they can disrupt current relationships, perpetuating cycles of fear and insecurity that may seem inescapable.

Let us consider how these emotional patterns from childhood wounds directly correlate with adult relationships. For instance, if, as a child, you experienced emotional neglect, you might have developed an acute sensitivity to the emotional availability of others. This sensitivity, although a rational adaptation to your childhood environment, can become problematic in adult relationships. It might manifest as hypervigilance regarding a partner's moods or behaviors, interpreting even minor withdrawals or mood changes as potential threats to the relationship. This state of heightened alert can lead to behaviors such as clinging or overly accommodating actions, which are efforts to secure emotional assurance from others, mirroring the unmet needs of your inner child.

Discuss the Cycle of Reactivity

Understanding the cycle of reactivity triggered by these old wounds is crucial for breaking free from them. In adult relationships, specific triggers—such as a partner's casual remark or a friend's inattention—can reactivate old fears and insecurities. This reactivation often leads to an automatic, intense emotional response that is disproportionate to the actual event. For example, a partner's distracted response might be perceived as neglect, triggering a flood of anxiety and fear similar to what was experienced in childhood. This emotional surge can compel you to react in ways that might be counterproductive, such as demanding reassurance or starting a conflict, essentially repeating historical patterns established in childhood.

Highlight the Role of Awareness

The pivotal role of awareness in this context cannot be overstated. Recognizing these patterns is the essential first step toward change. Awareness allows you to see the connections between past wounds and present reactions, providing a map of the emotional minefields that might otherwise sabotage your relationships. This awareness is not merely about intellectual understanding but involves cultivating a mindful presence that can observe these reactions without immediately acting on them. It's about noticing when you're feeling insecure or abandoned and pausing to consider if these feelings are truly reflective of the current situation or if they are echoes of the past.

Provide Insights from Therapy

Therapeutic practices offer profound insights into how addressing inner child wounds can transform adult relationships. Therapy provides a safe space to explore these wounds, to understand their origins, and to develop new, healthier ways of relating to oneself and others. Techniques such as cognitive-behavioral therapy (CBT) help in identifying and changing the thought patterns that perpetuate these cycles of reactivity. Dialectical Behavior Therapy (DBT) complements this by teaching skills for emotional regulation, distress tolerance, and mindfulness, which are particularly beneficial for those struggling with the intense emotions and fears that often accompany anxious attachment.

Meanwhile, therapies like psychodynamic therapy delve deeper into emotional patterns and childhood experiences, helping to heal the inner child directly. Many find that as they heal these wounds, their relationships become more secure and less driven by fear. They report greater stability and satisfaction in their connections, as they no longer react from a place of unhealed trauma but move from a foundation of healed and integrated experiences.

Through these therapeutic journeys, countless individuals have shifted from anxious attachment towards more secure ways of connecting, demonstrating that the chains of the past can be broken. Healing these deep-seated wounds not only improves personal well-being but fundamentally transforms the nature of one's relationships. As these old patterns dissolve, new possibilities for love, connection, and security emerge, allowing for relationships that are rich with trust and mutual respect rather than fraught with fear and misunderstanding. This transformation is not instantaneous but is a testament to the power of addressing the root causes of emotional distress and the capacity for profound change inherent in all of us.

TECHNIQUES TO COMMUNICATE WITH YOUR INNER CHILD

Communicating with your inner child is an essential aspect of healing and personal growth. This process allows you to address and nurture the part of yourself that still reacts with the fears, needs, and emotions of the child you once were. Various techniques, such as journaling, meditation, and dialoguing can facilitate this deep and meaningful communication. Each method provides a unique way to connect with your inner child, helping you to understand and heal the underlying issues contributing to your anxious attachment style.

Journaling is a powerful tool to begin dialoguing with your inner child. It offers a safe, private space where you can express thoughts and feelings that you might not be ready to share with others. Start by writing a letter to your inner child. Address the child you once were with compassion and understanding. Acknowledge their fears, soothe their pains, and validate their feelings. For example, you might write about a specific incident from your childhood that left you feeling abandoned or scared. Explain to your inner child how you, as an adult, understand and care about what they went through. This practice can be profoundly healing, as it helps to reprocess past traumas from a position of strength and maturity.

Meditation, particularly guided imagery, is another effective technique for connecting with your inner child. In a quiet, comfortable space, close your eyes and imagine a scene where you can meet your inner child. Visualize a safe, peaceful place—perhaps a garden or a cozy room—where your child feels secure. Picture yourself approaching the child, noticing their appearance and expressions. Speak to them with kindness, and listen to what they have to say. This mental dialogue can help you uncover the child's hidden fears and desires, providing insights into the roots of your current emotional struggles. Regular practice of this meditation can strengthen your relationship with your inner child, promoting inner peace and emotional resilience.

Dialoguing, either through journaling or meditation, can sometimes bring up intense emotions. It is crucial to create a safe emotional space where these feelings can be expressed without judgment. One way to ensure safety is to set clear intentions at the beginning of each session. Remind yourself that the purpose is not to relieve pain but to acknowledge and soothe it. You might find it helpful to have comforting objects nearby, such as soothing music, soft blankets, or even a comforting beverage, to help ground you if the emotions become overwhelming. Allow yourself to take breaks and return to the present moment if you start feeling too distressed. Remember, the goal is gentle healing, not re-traumatization.

Encouraging emotional honesty is vital when engaging with your inner child. Many of us have been conditioned to suppress or dismiss our feelings, especially those that are painful or uncomfortable. However, acknowledging and validating your inner child's emotions is crucial for healing. When you recognize and accept these feelings, you communicate to your inner child that their experiences are real and valid. This validation can be profoundly healing, helping to dissolve old wounds and build new foundations of trust and security within yourself. As you practice these techniques, focus on responding to your inner child as you would to a real child who is scared or hurt—with compassion, presence, and unconditional support.

Through these practices, you will develop a more in-depth understanding of yourself and a more compassionate approach to your emotions and reactions. This ongoing dialogue with your inner child can lead to significant transformations in how you relate to yourself and others, paving the way for more secure and fulfilling relationships. As you continue to engage with these techniques, you may find that the voice of your inner child becomes a powerful guide, leading you toward greater emotional freedom and authenticity in your life.

HEALING CHILDHOOD TRAUMA: THE FIRST STEPS

The path toward healing from childhood trauma is both profound and personal. It begins with the courageous act of recognition—acknowledging the presence and impact of trauma in your life. This initial step is often the hardest, as it involves confronting painful memories and emotions that you may have long tried to keep at bay. Recognizing trauma means looking squarely at those dark corners of your past and accepting that they have influenced who you are. But more importantly, it involves understanding that these experiences do not define your entire being or dictate your future. Admitting the pain is not about assigning blame or dwelling in victimhood; it's about reclaiming control over your emotional life by acknowledging your experiences and their impact on you.

As you embark on this journey, it's crucial to seek support. This can come in various forms—trusted friends, family members, support groups, or mental health professionals. Each offers a different kind of comfort and aid. Friends and family can provide a listening ear and a shoulder to lean on, while support groups offer the solidarity of shared experiences, helping you feel less isolated in your struggles. However, professional help often proves indispensable in effectively managing and healing from trauma. Therapists or counselors trained in trauma recovery can provide guided, evidence-based approaches to dealing with your emotional scars. They offer a safe space where you can explore your feelings without judgment, helping you to process and make sense of your past in ways that friends or family might not be equipped to do.

Professional therapy for trauma recovery often involves specific techniques that are designed to help you confront and process traumatic memories safely and constructively. Among these, Eye Movement Desensitization and Reprocessing (EMDR) and somatic experiencing are two of the most effective methods. EMDR involves the patient recalling distressing images while receiving one of several types of bilateral sensory input, such as side-to-side eye movements or hand tapping. This process is thought to lessen the emotional impact of memories, helping you to become less affected by the images and feelings associated with the trauma. Somatic experiencing, on the other hand, focuses on bodily sensations and aims to help you renegotiate and heal trauma rather than relive the painful events. Through gentle exercises and guidance, you learn to release and resolve the physical tension that remains in the aftermath of trauma.

The stories of those who have walked this path before you can serve as powerful motivation and provide a roadmap for your healing process. Take, for instance, the story of Michael, a middle-aged accountant who suffered from severe childhood neglect. For years, Michael struggled with deep-seated feelings of unworthiness and fear of abandonment, which affected his relationships and self-esteem. Through therapy, including EMDR and family therapy, he gradually learned to process his traumatic experiences and began to understand how they had shaped his views about himself and his relationships. As he worked through these issues, Michael found a new sense of self-worth and began to form healthier, more secure attachments in his relationships. His story is a testament to the transformative power of confronting and healing from one's past and is just one of the many examples of individuals who have reclaimed their emotional well-being through dedicated therapeutic work.

By engaging with these steps and techniques, you take crucial action towards healing not just your past but also in shaping a future where trauma does not hold sway over your emotional life. The road to recovery is neither straightforward nor easy, but it is paved with the promise of a more peaceful and fulfilling life.

FORGIVENESS AND RECONCILIATION WITH PAST HURTS

Forgiveness is often depicted as a pivotal moment of release in stories and films—a single, profound decision that frees the protagonist from the chains of past grievances. In reality, forgiveness is a more complex and nuanced journey, especially when it involves the deep-seated wounds of our inner child. For those grappling with anxious attachment, the act of forgiveness towards oneself and others isn't just about letting go of resentment; it's a crucial step in healing the parts of ourselves that remain trapped in past pain. It is about giving your inner child permission to move forward without the burden of unresolved anger and hurt.

Forgiving does not necessarily entail reconciliation with those who have caused us pain. This is an important distinction to understand. Forgiveness is an internal process that helps you find peace, release anger, and lessen the hold that past hurts have on your emotional health. It is about restoring your well-being, not necessarily mending a relationship. Reconciliation might follow forgiveness, but it is a separate decision that depends on many factors, including the willingness and capacity of both parties to rebuild trust. You can forgive someone and choose not to allow them back into your life. Conversely, you might decide to reconnect with someone if you believe it is safe and healthy to do so, but only after you have truly forgiven them.

The process of forgiving is complex and deeply personal, involving several stages that unfold over time. Initially, it requires you to recognize the hurt that you have suffered. This recognition is not about dwelling on the pain but about acknowledging its impact on your life. For instance, recognizing how a parent's neglect or criticism during your childhood has shaped your feelings of self-worth and your attachment style can be painful yet illuminating. Following this, understanding comes into play. This involves seeing the context of the hurt—perhaps recognizing the limitations or struggles of the person who hurt you, which, while not excusing their actions, can help you to see them in a more nuanced light.

Deciding to let go is perhaps the most challenging step. It involves an active choice to release the anger and resentment that may feel like your only protection against further emotional pain. Letting go is a commitment to stop letting these past hurts dictate how you feel and interact with the world. It's helpful to remember that forgiveness is not a betrayal of your past experiences but a reclaiming of your power over your present and future.

Personal reflection plays a vital role throughout the forgiveness process. It's beneficial to periodically reflect on your readiness to forgive and the potential benefits it might bring. Consider how holding on to anger and resentment has affected your life. Has it influenced your relationships, your self-esteem, or even your physical health? Reflecting on these questions can clarify your feelings and motivate you to engage more deeply with the process of forgiveness. For some, journaling these reflections can be particularly therapeutic, providing a private space to express and work through complex emotions.

As you navigate the terrain of forgiveness, remember that it is a process, not a one-time event. It might involve moving forward and then stepping back when old feelings resurface. This ebb and flow are normal. Each step forward, no matter how small, is a part of the journey toward healing your inner child and freeing yourself from the shadows of past hurts. By embarking on this path, you open up new possibilities for peace and happiness in your current life, unencumbered by the weight of old grievances.

INTERACTIVE EXERCISES TO RECONNECT WITH YOUR INNER CHILD

Engaging with your inner child can be a profoundly transformative experience, offering both healing and a renewed zest for life. To foster this connection, let's explore various interactive exercises designed to engage and celebrate the childlike aspects of your personality. These activities are crafted to make the process enjoyable, reminiscent of the carefree joy experienced in childhood, while providing deep psychological benefits.

One effective way to reconnect with your inner child is through drawing. This doesn't require any artistic skill but an openness to express yourself freely. Begin with a simple exercise: get some crayons or colored pencils and a large sheet of paper. Draw a picture of a place that made you feel safe or happy as a child. It could be a real place, like your childhood bedroom or a fantastical landscape from your imagination. As you draw, allow yourself to feel the crayon's texture against the paper and appreciate the colors blending together. This activity helps bring forward memories and feelings from your childhood, giving your adult self a visual and emotional glimpse into the world of your inner child.

Role-playing is another powerful tool for inner child work. This can be done alone or with a trusted friend or therapist. Set up a scenario that lets you embody your inner child, perhaps revisiting a particular moment from your childhood that was either significant or troublesome. Speak and act as you would have at that age, allowing yourself to express what you might not have been able to at the time. This exercise can be particularly liberating as it provides a safe space to voice previously unexpressed emotions and to experiment with altering the outcomes of past events, thereby instilling a sense of empowerment and resolution.

Dialoguing with your inner child can also be a profound exercise. Start by finding a quiet, comfortable place where you won't be disturbed. Close your eyes and picture your inner child. Ask them what they need from you right now. Do they need comfort, understanding, fun, or maybe protection? Allow them to answer and have a conversation as you would with a real child. This mental dialogue is crucial for understanding the needs of your inner child and can guide you on how to meet these needs in your current life.

Incorporating these exercises into your routine is essential for maintaining and deepening your connection with your inner child. Regular practice helps to solidify the relationship you're building and ensures that your inner child feels continually seen and valued. This ongoing engagement aids in healing and enhances your overall joy and vitality in life. Each exercise promises rediscovery and renewal, bringing to the forefront the parts of yourself that are waiting to be embraced with compassion and joy.

As you embark on these exercises, remember that the goal is to integrate the playful, innocent, and vulnerable parts of your inner child into your adult existence. This integration is not about returning to a state of childhood but about acknowledging and valuing all parts of your being, thereby fostering a fuller, more harmonious self. These exercises are stepping stones to a greater understanding of yourself and a more enriched, emotionally balanced life. They are designed to be accessible, requiring nothing more than your time, your honesty, and your willingness to engage with the deepest parts of yourself.

In conclusion, this chapter has explored various interactive exercises designed to help you reconnect with your inner child. By drawing, role-playing, and dialoguing, you engage in activities that not only evoke the essence of your childhood experiences but also facilitate a profound connection with your inner self. These practices are not only about revisiting the past but about bringing its best aspects into your present, enriching your emotional world, and enhancing your relationships. As you move forward, carry with you the joy, creativity, and openness of your inner child, allowing these qualities to infuse your daily life with a renewed sense of wonder and possibility.

Moving into the next chapter, we will build on these foundations, exploring deeper strategies for nurturing your inner child and integrating these practices into a holistic approach to personal growth and emotional healing. This journey is about reclaiming your full self, embracing both the joys and challenges of your past, and stepping into a future where your inner child and adult self walk hand in hand, each supporting and enriching the other.

OVERCOMING INSECURITY AND FEAR

W hen the echoes of past doubts and the shadows of old fears cloud your present, it can feel like walking through a maze with no clear exit. But imagine, just for a moment, that each step you take is guided by a newfound understanding of your own worth, armed with tools that not only illuminate the path but also fortify your resolve. This chapter is dedicated to that very transformation— from the grip of insecurity and fear to the solid ground of self-esteem and confidence. Here, we will explore how to cultivate a deep-seated sense of self-worth that stands firm against the challenges of anxious attachment and past relational experiences.

BUILDING SELF-ESTEEM: PRACTICES FOR INNER STRENGTH

Identify Sources of Low Self-Esteem

Your journey towards greater self-esteem begins with understanding its roots. Often, those with anxious attachment styles find their self-esteem intertwined with their early relational experiences. If, as a child, you felt your worth was measured by how much attention or affection you received, you might find yourself as an adult still looking for that validation, albeit subconsciously. This dependency on external validation for self-worth sets a fragile foundation, easily shaken by the slightest hint of disapproval or neglect.

Take a moment to reflect on how these early experiences might be influencing your current self-image. Consider the relationships that significantly impacted your perceptions of self-worth. Were there moments when you felt particularly valued or devalued? Understanding these influences is crucial, not for assigning blame but for recognizing patterns that may have led you to undervalue yourself. By bringing these patterns to light, you are already taking the first step towards transforming them.

Incorporate Strength-Based Approaches

Shifting the focus from perceived failures to personal strengths and accomplishments is a powerful strategy for rebuilding self-esteem. Begin by creating an inventory of your strengths. This can be qualities you admire about yourself or achievements you are proud of. Reflect on moments when you overcame a challenge or made a positive impact on someone else's life.

Engaging in this exercise allows you to see yourself in a new light. It may feel uncomfortable at first, especially if you're used to focusing on your weaknesses. However, this shift in perspective is essential for building a more balanced and compassionate view of yourself. Regularly updating and revisiting this inventory can serve as a constant reminder of your capabilities and worth, particularly during moments of doubt.

Promote Self-Compassion

Self-compassion is a nurturing practice that fosters kindness towards oneself, especially in instances of perceived inadequacy or failure. Begin by acknowledging that struggling with insecurity or fear is a part of being human. Then, integrate self-kindness affirmations into your daily routine. Phrases like "I am doing my best, and that is enough" or "I treat myself with kindness and patience" can be powerful antidotes to self-criticism.

Moreover, when you find yourself ruminating over past mistakes or fearing rejection, pause and ask yourself, "Would I speak to someone I love in this harsh, critical way?" If the answer is no, then consider how you might soften your approach to yourself. This practice reduces self-judgment and aligns your relationship with yourself to one of support and compassion.

Engage in Confidence-Building Activities

Building self-esteem involves not only changing how you see yourself but also how you carry yourself in the world. Engaging in activities that naturally build confidence is a key component of this process. For instance, public speaking is a powerful way to bolster self-assurance. Starting with small, informal groups and gradually working your way up can dramatically transform your confidence levels.

Similarly, joining hobby groups or learning new skills enhances your abilities and puts you in environments where you can receive positive feedback and support from others. These activities provide practical experiences that reinforce your sense of competence and achievement. Over time, as you collect more of these positive experiences, your self-esteem begins to build a new foundation, one that is rooted in genuine self-appreciation and robust confidence.

As you integrate these practices into your life, remember that the transformation of self-esteem is a gradual process. Each step you take is a building block in constructing a healthier, more secure sense of self. This chapter not only equips you with the tools to start this building process but also guides you through the practical application of these strategies, ensuring that you have a solid plan to move forward with confidence. As you continue to apply these techniques, you'll find that the shadow of insecurity becomes smaller, overshadowed by the growing light of self-assuredness and inner strength.

MANAGING FEAR OF ABANDONMENT IN DAILY LIFE

Navigating life with an undercurrent of abandonment fears can often feel like you're always waiting for the other shoe to drop. Every phone call not returned, every message unanswered, can seem like a prelude to a painful ending. Understanding and managing this fear effectively can open up a new way of experiencing relationships that are based on security rather than anxiety. To embark on this transformative path, the first step is to identify the specific triggers that stir up fears of abandonment. Triggers can vary widely but often involve situations where you feel excluded, neglected, or disconnected. For example, you might feel a surge of anxiety when your partner seems unusually quiet, interpreting their silence as a sign they're pulling away. Alternatively, seeing friends post on social media gatherings that you weren't invited to might evoke feelings of being left out or unwanted. Recognizing these triggers is crucial because it allows you to respond proactively rather than reactively.

Once you have a clear understanding of what triggers your fear of abandonment, developing coping strategies becomes the next critical step. Grounding techniques can be particularly effective in these moments. These techniques help divert your mind from spiraling anxieties and bring your focus to the present moment. One simple method is the 5-4-3-2-1 technique, which involves identifying five things you can see, four you can touch, three you can hear, two you can smell, and one you can taste. This method not only helps anchor your senses to the here and now but also diffuses the intensity of the emotional response you're experiencing. Breathing exercises also play a key role in calming the nervous system. Practices like deep diaphragmatic breathing can help reduce the physiological symptoms of anxiety, such as rapid heartbeat and shallow breathing, thus making the fear more manageable.

Building or strengthening your support system is another cornerstone in managing fears of abandonment. A robust support network can provide the emotional assurance and validation needed to counter feelings of insecurity. Reach out to friends or family members who understand your struggles and are willing to provide the emotional comfort you need. It's important these individuals are not only supportive but also reliable, as consistency from your support network reinforces a sense of security and belonging. Communicate openly with them about your fears and how they can help you feel more secure. Whether it's a reassuring text during a stressful day or a regular check-in call, these small gestures can make a significant difference in alleviating your fears.

Planning for triggering events is also essential, especially in situations where you anticipate potential triggers. If you know, for example, that your partner's upcoming business trip might stir your fears of abandonment, discuss this with them ahead of time. Express your concerns and establish ways they can help maintain a sense of connection with you while they're away, like scheduled calls or texts. Similarly, setting clear expectations before attending social events can help manage anxieties about inclusion and acceptance. Perhaps agree on a signal with a friend that means you need extra support or a moment to regroup. Being proactive helps in managing immediate anxieties and builds a framework within which you can feel more secure, gradually easing the overarching fear of abandonment.

While simple in concept, these strategies require persistence and courage to implement effectively. Each step taken is a move towards not just managing fear but reclaiming your ability to engage in relationships with confidence and peace. As you continue to apply these techniques, you'll likely discover not only a decrease in your fear of abandonment but also an increase in your overall emotional resilience, paving the way for more fulfilling and stable relationships.

TRANSFORMING FEAR INTO SECURITY: A TRANSFORMATIVE GUIDE

Transforming the pervasive fear of abandonment into a fortified sense of security isn't merely a flip of a switch but a progressive journey that unfolds through deliberate steps and strategies. The process begins by setting small, achievable goals that serve as stepping stones toward the larger objective of emotional stability. These goals could range from initiating a difficult conversation with a partner to spending an evening alone without feeling anxious. The key is to start small—each goal should challenge your comfort zone but still be attainable enough to avoid overwhelming you. As you achieve these goals, you build a foundation of success that boosts your confidence and reinforces your sense of control over your fears.

This structured approach is complemented by the practice of incremental exposure, a technique widely used in therapeutic settings to help individuals gradually confront their fears. The idea is to slowly expose yourself to the situations that trigger your fear of abandonment but in a controlled and manageable way. For instance, if waiting for a text message from your partner triggers anxiety, you might start by setting a realistic expectation to not check your phone for fifteen minutes. Gradually, as your tolerance increases, you could extend this time. During these exposure sessions, it's crucial to employ coping techniques such as deep breathing or mindfulness to manage anxiety. Over time, this practice helps reduce the intensity of your fear response, making it more manageable and less disruptive.

Understanding the psychological roots of fear plays a pivotal role in transforming it. Fear, especially fear of abandonment, often stems from early life experiences where emotional needs were not met. By understanding this, you can begin to see your fear not as a part of your identity but as a natural response to past circumstances. This shift in perspective is crucial, as it allows you to detach from the fear and approach it with curiosity rather than dread. Exploring the origins of your fear demystifies it and empowers you to address it with informed strategies rather than reactive emotions. This understanding encourages a compassionate self-view that acknowledges your fear as a valid response but not an unchangeable one.

. . .

Facilitate Reflective Journaling

Reflective journaling is a powerful tool to solidify the gains from these practices. Regularly writing down your fears, experiences, and the steps you're taking to manage them helps in several ways. First, it provides a tangible record of your progress, which can be amazingly encouraging on days when it feels like you're not making headway. Each entry acts as a milestone in your journey towards security. Additionally, journaling fosters a deeper, more introspective relationship with your emotions. It encourages you to explore and express your feelings in a safe, private space, which can lead to new insights and resolutions.

Plan to journal at least once a week, focusing on what fears were most present, how you coped with them, and what you learned from the experiences. Be sure to include any exposure exercises you attempted and their outcomes. Did the anxiety decrease over time? How did you feel after confronting a fear-inducing situation? What coping strategies were most effective? Answering these questions not only aids in processing your experiences but also prepares you for future challenges by highlighting what works best for you.

As you engage with this step-by-step guide, remember that transforming fear into security is a gradual process that requires patience, persistence, and self-compassion. Each step forward, no matter how small, is a significant stride towards a life where fear no longer holds the reins. With each achieved goal, each exposure exercise, and each journal entry, you are actively constructing a new paradigm of emotional resilience and security. This transformation, though challenging, is deeply rewarding, paving the way for relationships built on trust and stability, free from the shadows of past fears.

TECHNIQUES FOR EMOTIONAL REGULATION AND ANXIETY REDUCTION

In the intricate dance of managing our emotions, especially when they seem as tumultuous as ocean waves during a storm, finding the right techniques to maintain your composure can feel like discovering a hidden treasure. Emotional regulation is not about suppressing your feelings but understanding and channeling them in ways that serve you better. Emotional awareness training is one such technique that invites you to become an observant rather than a reactive participant in your emotional experiences. This involves recognizing and naming your emotions as they arise, examining their triggers, and acknowledging their impact without immediate judgment or action. This heightened awareness creates a space between feeling and action, allowing you to choose responses that align more closely with your values and goals.

Reappraisal is another powerful strategy in the toolkit of emotional regulation. It involves changing the way you think about a situation that has caused you distress. For example, if you're feeling anxious about a forthcoming public speaking engagement, instead of thinking, "I'm going to embarrass myself," you could reappraise the situation by considering it as an opportunity to share your knowledge and passion with others. This shift in perspective can reduce anxiety and increase feelings of control and competence. Acceptance, on the other hand, involves acknowledging your emotions for what they are without trying to change them. This can be particularly useful for emotions that are resistant to change or situations that are beyond your control. By accepting your feelings, you reduce the struggle against them and conserve emotional energy that can be used more constructively elsewhere.

The journey towards emotional regulation also involves mastering certain anxiety reduction techniques that can soothe your nervous system and bring about a sense of calm. Progressive muscle relaxation, for instance, can be a potent tool. This technique involves tensing and then relaxing different muscle groups in your body. The contrast between tension and relaxation helps to highlight feelings of relaxation, making you more aware of physical sensations and diverting your focus from anxiety-provoking thoughts. Guided imagery enhances this experience by encouraging you to visualize a peaceful scene, perhaps a quiet beach or a serene forest, which engages your mind in a calming narrative.

Deep breathing exercises are equally foundational. By focusing on slow, deep breaths, you stimulate the parasympathetic nervous system, which helps reduce the physiological symptoms of anxiety, such as rapid heartbeat and shallow breathing. Techniques like the 4-7-8 breathing method, where you inhale for four seconds, hold your breath for seven seconds, and exhale for eight seconds, can be particularly effective. When practiced regularly, this helps manage acute anxiety and contributes to long-term anxiety reduction.

Integrating these techniques into your daily activities ensures they become part of your routine, transforming them from conscious practices to automatic responses that you can draw upon as needed. Begin by setting aside specific times in your day for practice, such as during morning routines or in the evening before bed. Over time, as these practices become more ingrained, you will find it increasingly natural to employ them in situations where you are triggered. This habitual integration acts as both a preventative measure and an immediate remedy to emotional upheaval, anchoring you more firmly in emotional stability.

To truly gauge the effectiveness of these emotional regulation and anxiety reduction strategies, it's beneficial to measure your emotional improvement objectively. Tools like mood diaries or anxiety scales can be invaluable here. By regularly recording your emotional states and the circumstances that trigger them, you can start to see patterns and track changes over time. This not only provides insight into which strategies are most effective for you but also reinforces the progress you're making, which can be amazingly motivating. Mood diaries should be simple to maintain, focusing on daily entries that record key emotions, the context in which they arose, and the techniques you used to manage them. Over weeks and months, this record will serve as a testament to your growing ability to regulate your emotions and manage anxiety, guiding you toward a life where feelings of fear and insecurity do not overwhelm your capacity to enjoy life and engage with others meaningfully.

THE POWER OF MINDFULNESS IN COMBATING INSECURITY

Mindfulness, a practice rooted in ancient tradition yet strikingly relevant to modern psychological health, revolves around cultivating a deep, non-judgmental awareness of the present moment. At its core, mindfulness involves observing your current experiences—thoughts, feelings, bodily sensations—without trying to alter, judge, or overly engage with them. This practice teaches you to notice your mental and emotional processes in a way that is detached and objective, which can significantly alter your relationship with your thoughts, particularly those that might contribute to feelings of insecurity and fear.

For individuals grappling with anxious attachment, mindfulness offers a powerful tool to manage the overwhelming emotions that often accompany fears of abandonment. By practicing mindfulness, you learn to sit with uncomfortable feelings without immediately reacting to them. This can be profoundly freeing, as it interrupts the habitual responses of anxiety, such as clinging or seeking reassurance, allowing you to choose more constructive behaviors instead. Furthermore, mindfulness enhances emotional resilience by fostering a greater tolerance for emotional discomfort, gradually reducing the intensity of emotional reactions, and helping you respond to relationship challenges with greater calm and clarity.

To integrate mindfulness into your life, you might begin with mindfulness meditation practices. One foundational practice is mindful breathing, which you can do virtually anywhere, at any time. Simply focus your attention on the sensation of your breath as it enters and leaves your body. Notice the rise and fall of your chest, the feeling of air passing through your nostrils, and the slight pause between inhalation and exhalation. Whenever your mind wanders—and it will—gently acknowledge where it went, then bring your focus back to your breath. This practice calms the mind and trains you in the art of returning your attention to the present moment, which is crucial for managing anxiety and insecurity.

Another effective mindfulness exercise is the body scan. This involves slowly moving your attention through different parts of your body, observing any sensations, tension, or discomfort you might feel. Start at the top of your head and gradually work your way down to your toes. The key here is observation without judgment. If you notice tension in your shoulders, for example, simply acknowledge its presence without trying to relax the muscle. Through body scans, you become more attuned to your body's responses, which can be particularly useful for recognizing the physical manifestations of anxiety and insecurity.

Mindfulness can be particularly beneficial for those dealing with anxious attachment, as it directly addresses the hyper-reactivity to perceived threats of abandonment. By staying present and grounded, you are less likely to spiral into anxiety when a loved one is distant or when you face relational uncertainties. Regular mindfulness practice helps shift your focus from fear-based narratives about your relationships to a more balanced perspective that recognizes these narratives as just one possible interpretation of events, not an absolute reality.

To reap the full benefits of mindfulness, consistency is key. Integrating mindfulness into your daily routine ensures that it becomes a stable part of your mental health toolkit. You might set aside a few minutes each morning for a sitting of meditation or use mindfulness apps that guide you through exercises. Additionally, community classes can offer support and structure for your practice, connecting you with others who are on a similar path and reinforcing your commitment to mindfulness. These resources aid in regular practice and enrich your understanding of mindfulness, providing a broader context and more in-depth insight into how this ancient practice can be a modern remedy for the emotional challenges of anxious attachment.

As you continue to explore and practice mindfulness, you will likely discover an increasing sense of peace and stability within yourself. This tranquility is a direct result of your ability to manage thoughts and emotions more effectively, ensuring they do not overrun your present experiences or future possibilities. Mindfulness opens up a space where fear and insecurity have less influence, allowing you to engage with life and your relationships with a newfound clarity and calm.

CREATING PERSONAL AFFIRMATIONS FOR SELF-ASSURANCE

The practice of using affirmations might seem simple, yet it wields the power to transform deeply ingrained patterns of thought and emotion. Affirmations are not just positive statements; they are declarations of intent, self-worth, and the truth as you choose to see and create it. For those dealing with fears of abandonment and issues of self-worth linked to anxious attachment, affirmations can serve as powerful tools to reshape thought processes and strengthen emotional resilience.

Crafting effective, personalized affirmations begins with identifying the core beliefs that you hold about yourself and your relationships. These might include negative beliefs like "I am not worthy of love" or "I will always be abandoned." The goal is to transform these into positive, empowering statements that reinforce your value and security. For example, "I am worthy of love and respect" or "I am creating secure and loving relationships in my life." When creating these affirmations, it's crucial that they resonate with you deeply and are stated in the present tense, as if they are already true. This helps to embed these concepts into your subconscious, gradually altering your internal narrative.

The psychology behind affirmations lies in their ability to rewire our brain's thought patterns. Regular repetition of these positive statements can shift your focus from negative, self-limiting beliefs to positive, self-enhancing beliefs. Neuroscientific research supports this, showing that affirmations can stimulate the areas of the brain associated with self-related processing and reward, similar to how we might feel when we achieve a significant goal. This neural activation reinforces the acceptance of these affirmations as truth, gradually diminishing the hold of old, negative beliefs.

To weave affirmations effectively into your daily life, consider incorporating them into your morning routine or your meditation sessions. Morning affirmations can set a positive tone for the day, fortifying your mindset against insecurities and fears that might arise. You might repeat affirmations like "Today, I choose to see the best in myself and others" while you're having your morning coffee or during your commute. Alternatively, integrating affirmations into meditation can deepen their impact, as the relaxed state of mind you achieve in meditation makes your subconscious more receptive. Visual reminders can also be profoundly effective. Placing sticky notes with affirmations on your bathroom mirror, computer monitor, or fridge can serve as frequent, uplifting prompts throughout your day.

The success of affirmations in boosting self-assurance and mitigating attachment-related fears is not just theoretical but is backed by numerous personal testimonies. Consider the story of Ella, a graphic designer who struggled with low self-esteem and anxiety in her relationships. By integrating affirmations like "I am capable of healthy, stable love" into her daily journaling and meditation, she noticed a significant boost in her confidence and a decrease in her anxiety over time. She reported feeling more secure in her relationship and more resilient when facing setbacks. Ella's experience is a testament to how the consistent use of affirmations can lead to profound emotional and relational changes.

As you adopt this practice, remember that consistency is key. Affirmations are most effective when they are used regularly and with conviction. Over time, you will likely notice a shift in how you view yourself and your relationships, moving from a place of insecurity and fear to one of confidence and trust. This transformation, facilitated by your own words and beliefs, empowers you to engage more fully and joyfully with life and with the people you care about.

By focusing on this powerful tool, you've equipped yourself with another key element in overcoming the challenges of anxious attachment. As we conclude this chapter, remember the journey you've embarked on through these pages is about reinforcing your inner strength and reshaping your emotional landscape. The techniques and insights shared here are stepping stones to a more secure and self-assured you, providing a foundation upon which healthier relationships can be built.

Looking ahead, the next chapter will delve into deeper strategies for sustaining these gains, ensuring that the progress you make is maintained and built upon as you continue to grow and thrive in your emotional and relational life. Through a combination of ongoing practices and new techniques to explore, you will discover how to solidify your newfound confidence and security, ensuring they become permanent fixtures in your life's journey.

4

DEVELOPING HEALTHY
COMMUNICATION SKILLS

Communication stands at the heart of human connection, an intricate dance that can uplift or undermine our relationships. Yet, for those grappling with anxious attachment, the rhythm of this dance can sometimes feel off-beat, marked by missteps and misunderstandings that stem from unspoken fears and unhealed wounds. This chapter is dedicated to refining your communication skills, transforming them into tools that foster understanding, respect, and closeness rather than conflict and distance. Here, we delve into the art of assertive communication—a style that maintains your dignity while respecting others, proving essential for building healthier, more secure relationships.

THE ART OF ASSERTIVE COMMUNICATION

Define Assertiveness

Assertiveness is a communication style that is both respectful and straightforward. It allows you to express your thoughts, feelings, and needs directly, clearly, and respectfully without infringing on the rights of others. This style stands in contrast to passive communication, where you might withhold your true thoughts to avoid conflict, and aggressive communication, where you advocate for your needs in a way that can be disrespectful or dismissive of others. There's also passive-aggressive communication, where your words might not directly convey your discontent, but your tone and actions do—an indirect approach that can confuse and erode trust.

Assertiveness is crucial in relationships because it balances honesty with empathy, creating a space where both parties feel valued and heard. It's about finding your voice and using it to bridge understanding rather than build walls. For those with a history of anxious attachment, mastering assertiveness can be particularly transformative, providing a way to express needs and fears without fear of abandonment or confrontation.

Teach Assertive Language

The essence of assertive communication lies in its unique language, which is pivotal for its effective practice. This language predominantly utilizes "I" statements, strategically focusing on articulating your feelings and experiences without casting blame or criticism toward others. For example, rather than resorting to accusations like, "You never listen to me," adopting an assertive stance would transform this into, "I feel upset when I perceive that my words are not being heard." This nuanced alteration does more than merely prevent the other party from becoming defensive; it actively fosters a conduit for authentic understanding and resolution. By weaving phrases such as "I need," "I feel," or "I would appreciate" into the dialogue, the conversation originates from a place of vulnerability and sincerity. This approach has the power to disarm potential conflict and promote a sense of reciprocity. The shift to expressing personal experiences and needs serves as an invitation for your conversational partner to step into your perspective without feeling under attack. This method facilitates a more respectful exchange and encourages a deeper mutual understanding and connection, laying the groundwork for healthier, more fulfilling relationships. Role-Playing Exercises

Role-playing is an effective method to practice assertive communication in a controlled, low-risk environment. These exercises can be particularly beneficial if you're not accustomed to speaking up or find yourself frequently overwhelmed in confrontational situations. For example, you could role-play asking for a raise with a colleague or friend acting as your boss. In this scenario, you might express your request by saying, "I would like to discuss my performance and the possibility of a raise. I feel my achievements and commitment over the past year have contributed significantly to the team, and I would appreciate consideration for a salary adjustment."

Similarly, discussing relationship needs with a partner in a role-play setting before addressing them in real life can help you refine your approach and gain confidence. The safe space created by role-playing allows you to experiment with different ways of expressing your needs and to receive feedback in a constructive manner.

Discuss the Benefits

The benefits of assertive communication extend beyond immediate interactions. It fosters deeper respect and understanding in relationships, helping to build a foundation of trust and openness. Real-life success stories underscore its impact; consider the case of a young woman who, through learning to communicate assertively, transformed her relationship with her partner. Previously, her fears of abandonment led her to either cling desperately or withdraw completely at signs of conflict. By adopting assertive communication, she started expressing her fears and needs without blame, which reduced her anxiety and deepened her connection with her partner, creating a more secure and satisfying relationship.

In essence, assertive communication equips you with the skills to express yourself openly and respectfully, paving the way for more honest and enriching interactions. As you integrate these practices into your daily life, you'll likely find that not only do your relationships improve, but your self-esteem and personal dignity grow stronger, creating a virtuous cycle of positive self-expression and connection.

HOW TO EXPRESS NEEDS WITHOUT FEAR

Expressing personal needs in various relationships can often feel like navigating a tightrope. On one side, there's the fear of rejection—the worry that your honest expressions might push others away. On the other, there's the anxiety about being a burden—this nagging thought that your needs are too much for others. These fears aren't just emotional hurdles; they're deeply rooted in our psychological makeup, often tied to past experiences where expressing needs might have led to disappointment or criticism. Understanding these fears is the first step towards overcoming them. It's about recognizing that these anxieties stem from a protective instinct—to keep ourselves safe from emotional pain. However, this protection also sets us off from genuine intimacy and connection, which fundamentally rely on the open exchange of personal needs and desires.

To navigate past these fears, one effective strategy is gradual exposure. Start by expressing smaller, less vulnerable needs to build up your confidence. For instance, you might ask a friend to choose a quieter restaurant to accommodate your preference for a less bustling environment, or you could ask your partner for help with household chores when you're feeling overwhelmed. These smaller requests can act as practice runs, gradually desensitizing you to the anxiety of asking for more significant needs down the line. Each positive outcome, where your needs are acknowledged and met, reinforces the belief that your voice deserves to be heard and that your needs are not burdens but legitimate requests.

Preparing emotionally before expressing more significant needs can also significantly impact how confidently you communicate. Techniques like deep breathing or positive visualization can be particularly beneficial. Take a moment to center yourself with deep, steady breaths before initiating the conversation. This helps calm the nervous system and clears your mind, allowing you to articulate your needs more clearly. Visualization, on the other hand, involves picturing the conversation going well, which can boost your confidence and reduce anxiety. Imagine the person listening attentively and responding kindly. This mental rehearsal primes you for a positive interaction, setting the stage for a constructive exchange.

Let's consider some practical examples to demonstrate effective communication of needs across different types of relationships. In a family setting, where dynamics can be complex, clarity and directness are your allies. Suppose you're feeling overwhelmed by family obligations and need more time for yourself. You might say, "I love spending time with the family, but I've been feeling stretched thin lately. I need to set aside one weekend a month for myself to recharge. I hope you can support me in this." This statement clearly communicates your need without blaming anyone for your feelings, making it easier for your family to understand and support your request.

Maintaining a balance of give-and-take in friendships is essential. If you feel you're always the one lending a listening ear, you might express your need for reciprocity. You could say, "I strongly value our talks and how I can support you. Lately, I've been going through some things too, and I'd really appreciate being able to share and get your support as well." This approach expresses your needs and reinforces the value you find in the friendship, encouraging a more balanced relationship.

In romantic relationships, expressing needs can feel particularly vulnerable but is crucial for deepening intimacy. If you need more verbal affirmation from your partner, you might express this need by saying, "I feel loved when you tell me you appreciate me or love me. It's something I need regularly to feel secure in our relationship. Could we work on expressing our appreciation for each other more often?" This kind of vulnerable sharing invites your partner into your emotional world and shows them specific ways they can help meet your emotional needs.

Each of these scenarios illustrates how tailored communication strategies can effectively address and express needs in various relationships. By practicing these techniques, you gradually build the confidence and skills needed to navigate the vulnerability of expressing personal needs. This enhances your relationships and fortifies your sense of self-worth and agency as you learn to advocate for yourself and your needs in a healthy, constructive manner.

HANDLING CONFLICT WITH CONFIDENCE AND CALM

Conflict is an inevitable part of relationships, whether romantic, familial, or professional. However, the way you manage these conflicts can dramatically affect your relationships' health and your own emotional well-being. It's not just about resolving disagreements but doing so in a way that strengthens trust and understanding. To navigate conflicts with confidence and calm, it's crucial to develop effective conflict resolution skills. These include understanding how to negotiate, finding common ground, and ensuring that both parties feel heard and respected.

Negotiation is a key skill in conflict resolution. It involves give-and-take, where both parties discuss their needs and desires and work toward a solution that is acceptable to both. The essence of successful negotiation lies in the ability to see the situation from the other person's perspective as well as your own. This doesn't mean you have to agree with their viewpoint, but understanding it can help you find common ground. Common ground is that mutual territory where both parties' needs overlap. Identifying this can de-escalate the conflict and lead to solutions that are sustainable and satisfying for everyone involved. For instance, if you and your partner are arguing about spending too much time apart, the common ground might be your mutual desire to strengthen the relationship. Recognizing this can shift the conversation from blame to collaboration, focusing on how both can adjust their schedules to spend more quality time together.

The setting and timing of when you choose to address a conflict are just as important as what you say. Engaging in a heated discussion when one or both of you are already stressed or tired is unlikely to be productive. Instead, choose a time when both of you are calm and can devote your full attention to the conversation. The setting should be private and free from distractions, providing a safe space where both parties feel comfortable expressing their thoughts and feelings. For example, discussing a sensitive issue like financial planning is best done at home, perhaps at a table where both can sit comfortably rather than in a public place or during a family gathering.

Maintaining calm and composure during conflict is essential. It's easy to let emotions get the best of you during heated discussions, but losing your temper can quickly escalate the situation. Practicing emotional regulation techniques such as taking deep breaths or pausing the conversation can help. If you feel your emotions rising, suggest taking a brief time-out. A few minutes apart can allow both parties to cool down, reflect on what they really want to communicate, and return to the discussion with a clearer perspective. This approach prevents the conflict from escalating and shows a commitment to resolving the issue respectfully.

Practicing these skills can be enhanced through role-playing scenarios, which allow you to develop and refine your conflict resolution strategies in a low-stress environment. For example, you could role-play a scenario with a friend where you must negotiate who will take on certain responsibilities at home. One might start by expressing their feelings using "I" statements like, "I feel overwhelmed when I have to manage all the household chores on my own." The other can practice finding common ground and suggesting compromises, such as alternating cooking days or setting a schedule for chores. These role-plays will help you build skills and boost your confidence in handling conflicts as they arise in real life.

By integrating these techniques into your communication repertoire, you equip yourself with the tools necessary to handle conflicts in ways that build rather than break relationships. Each conflict then becomes an opportunity to enhance mutual understanding and trust, paving the way for more meaningful and supportive connections. As you continue to practice these skills, you'll find that your ability to navigate disputes with calm and confidence naturally improves, reflecting positively on all areas of your life where communication plays a key role.

THE ROLE OF ACTIVE LISTENING IN ENHANCING CONNECTION

Active listening is a skill that transforms ordinary interactions into bridges of empathy and understanding. It involves fully concentrating on, understanding, responding to, and then remembering what the other person is saying. In the realm of building secure and healthy relationships, especially for those overcoming the challenges of anxious attachment, mastering active listening can be particularly transformative. It allows you to hear not just the words another person says but also to understand the complete message being conveyed. This skill is crucial in fostering a sense of emotional safety for both speakers and listeners, making it an essential component of effective communication.

The techniques of active listening are simple yet powerful. One fundamental technique is mirroring, which involves repeating back or paraphrasing what the other person has said to confirm understanding. This does not mean simply regurgitating their words but reflecting the core message, ensuring that you have indeed grasped their meaning. For example, if a partner expresses dissatisfaction about spending too little time together, you might respond with, "It sounds like you're feeling left out of our recent schedules. What can we do to improve this?" This response shows that you are listening and engaging with their concerns.

Affirmation stands as a pivotal technique in the art of active listening, where the act of validating the emotions or thoughts shared by another is paramount. It embodies a gesture of respect and acknowledges the courage it takes for someone to express their feelings or perspectives. This technique can be as straightforward yet profound as responding with, "I truly appreciate you opening up to me about this," or "I can see how that situation could make you feel that way." By affirming the other's experiences and emotions, you are essentially laying the foundation for deeper trust and emotional intimacy. Such affirmations are more than mere responses; they are powerful affirmations of the other person's value and the legitimacy of their feelings. This validation is a critical component of empathetic communication, signaling to the other person that their inner world is not only recognized but also respected. Consequently, this practice significantly fortifies the bonds of trust and emotional intimacy, marking a critical step towards nurturing secure and understanding relationships.

Summarizing can also enhance understanding and show that you are paying attention. It involves giving a brief restatement of the main points discussed in a conversation, especially at the end of a discussion. This technique not only confirms that you have understood all key information but also helps clarify any misunderstandings before they escalate into conflicts. For instance, at the end of a discussion about holiday plans, you might say, "So, we've agreed to visit your family for the first part of the holidays and then spend the rest with mine. Does that sound right?"

Interactive listening exercises can be amazingly effective for putting these techniques into practice. These exercises can be done with a partner or in groups and involve intentional practice of the techniques discussed. One such exercise is the repetition drill, where you ask a partner to speak about a topic for a few minutes and then try to repeat the key points back to them. This exercise helps in honing your summarizing skills and improves your ability to concentrate and remember details from conversations.

Active listening profoundly impacts relationships. It creates a space where all parties feel heard and understood, which is fundamental to resolving conflicts and deepening connections. Consider the case of a couple who were on the brink of separation due to chronic misunderstandings. Through counseling, they learned and practiced active listening skills, which transformed their communication pattern. They began to feel more connected and understood each other's needs better, which significantly improved their relationship quality. Their story is just one of many that highlights how active listening can turn communication breakdowns into opportunities for growth and closer connection.

Incorporating active listening into your daily interactions can thus be a game-changer, particularly for those working through anxious attachment styles. It reassures you that your voice is valued, and by offering the same consideration to others, you foster an environment of mutual respect and understanding. As these skills become a natural part of your communication repertoire, you'll find that your relationships are not only smoother but also richer and more rewarding.

NEGOTIATING BOUNDARIES IN RELATIONSHIPS

Understanding and setting healthy boundaries is akin to drawing a personal map that outlines your comfort zones, limits, and expectations in relationships. Boundaries are essential for maintaining both your well-being and the health of your relationships. They serve as guidelines for how you want to be treated by others, what you are willing and not willing to tolerate, and how you interact with people. Think of boundaries not as walls but as gateways that foster mutual respect and ensure that your relationships are based on genuine understanding and consent.

Setting boundaries effectively starts with self-reflection. It's important to first understand your own needs and limits. What makes you feel comfortable and safe? What values are non-negotiable for you in relationships? Reflecting on these questions can help you define your boundaries clearly. For instance, if personal space is crucial for your mental health, setting a boundary around how often you prefer to socialize—even with close friends—can help you maintain your well-being. Communicating these boundaries clearly and respectfully to others is the next step. Use direct and simple language that leaves no room for ambiguity. For example, you might say to a friend, "I value our time together, but I need some quiet evenings to myself during the week. Let's plan our get-togethers on weekends."

Enforcing boundaries is perhaps the most challenging part, especially if others are used to you having more lenient limits. It involves not only reiterating your boundaries when they are crossed but also taking action to uphold them. If a friend repeatedly ignores your requests for space, you might need to decline invitations more firmly or reduce the frequency of your interactions to protect your needs. This step often requires courage and consistency but is crucial for your long-term happiness and the health of your relationships.

Negotiating boundaries can be particularly nuanced in relationships with significant others. It often involves balancing closeness with personal independence. For example, you might agree on checking in with each other once a day when you're apart but respect that excessive calls or texts can feel overbearing. In professional contexts, boundaries might relate to maintaining a clear line between work and personal life, such as not answering work emails during family time or on weekends.

Addressing common challenges in setting boundaries is crucial. Many people worry that setting boundaries might seem selfish or that it will upset others. It's important to recognize that setting boundaries is a form of self-respect and an act of self-care—it's not about being selfish. If someone reacts negatively to your boundaries, it often reflects their own issues with limits and control, not a problem with your request. Communicating why these boundaries are important to you can help others understand your perspective better, making it easier for them to respect your needs.

Maintaining boundaries over time requires regular self-reflection and open communication. Life changes, and so might your needs and boundaries. Regularly checking in with yourself and reassessing your boundaries ensures they still serve your best interests. Additionally, open communication with those around you about your changing needs can help prevent misunderstandings and respect your evolving boundaries.

For instance, as your relationship with a partner deepens, you might feel comfortable relaxing some boundaries while tightening others. Discussing these changes openly can strengthen trust and mutual respect. Similarly, in a professional setting, as you take on new roles or responsibilities, your boundaries around work hours or task delegation might need adjustment. Regular discussions with your supervisor and colleagues can ensure that these new boundaries are respected, enabling you to perform effectively without burnout.

By understanding, setting, and maintaining clear boundaries, you protect your personal space and well-being and invite healthier, more respectful interactions with others. As you navigate through these processes, remember that boundaries aren't barriers. They are the expressions of your self-respect and commitment to fostering deeply satisfying and mutually respectful relationships.

ROLE-PLAYING SCENARIOS FOR COMMUNICATION PRACTICE

Role-playing exercises are a dynamic and effective way to sharpen your communication skills, providing a safe environment to explore and resolve common relational challenges. By stepping into structured scenarios, you can practice articulating your thoughts and feelings, learn to navigate difficult conversations, and improve your overall ability to communicate in various situations. Let's delve into developing detailed scenarios that cover typical communication challenges, such as expressing dissatisfaction or asking for help, which are essential skills for maintaining healthy, balanced relationships.

Creating detailed scenarios involves identifying common communication challenges that you might face in your day-to-day interactions. Imagine you are in a situation where you need to express dissatisfaction with a friend who has repeatedly canceled plans at the last minute. The scenario could start with you detailing the specific instances to your friend and expressing how these actions made you feel disregarded and unimportant. In developing this scenario, it's crucial to focus on using "I" statements to convey your feelings without casting blame, such as, "I feel hurt when plans are canceled abruptly as it makes me feel like my time isn't valued." This type of scenario teaches you to express your dissatisfaction clearly and respectfully, fostering a dialogue that can lead to understanding and change rather than conflict and resentment.

Incorporating role reversal in these exercises offers a powerful tool for empathy and understanding. By stepping into the shoes of another person, you gain insight into their perspective, which can illuminate why they may behave in certain ways. For instance, in the aforementioned scenario, switching roles and adopting the perspective of the friend who cancels plans might reveal underlying reasons for their behavior, such as work stress or personal issues. This exercise not only broadens your understanding but also fosters empathy, making it easier to find mutually acceptable solutions to conflicts.

Feedback is another integral component of role-playing. Learning how to give and receive constructive feedback can significantly enhance your communication skills. After a role-playing exercise, participants can discuss what was effective and what could be improved. For example, feedback might highlight the use of positive body language, such as maintaining eye contact, which makes the interaction feel more engaging and sincere. Alternatively, it might suggest areas for improvement, such as moderating tone to avoid sounding accusatory. This feedback loop is crucial for continuous improvement and helps refine your communication skills over time.

Encouraging group participation in these role-playing exercises can vastly enhance their effectiveness. Engaging friends or family members in these scenarios provides a more realistic and dynamic practice environment. Each participant brings their own perceptions and styles to the exercise, adding complexity and depth to the interaction. This diversity can challenge you to adapt your communication strategies in real time, closely mimicking real-life interactions. Group role-playing can be particularly beneficial in understanding and practicing communication dynamics in various types of relationships, from personal to professional.

Through these role-playing exercises, you are equipped not only to handle common communication challenges more effectively but also to strengthen your overall interpersonal skills. These scenarios encourage you to think critically about how you communicate and provide practical experience in managing real-world issues. As you become more proficient in navigating these exercises, you'll find that your confidence in handling difficult conversations in your everyday life significantly improves, leading to deeper and more fulfilling relationships.

As we wrap up this chapter on developing healthy communication skills, it's evident how essential clear and effective communication is to nurturing and sustaining relationships. The techniques and strategies explored, from assertive communication to role-playing exercises, provide a robust framework for enhancing your interpersonal interactions. These skills are not just tools for resolving conflicts or expressing needs; they are foundational elements that can transform the quality of your connections with others, making them richer and more resilient.

Looking ahead, the next chapter will build upon these communication skills by exploring strategies for fostering secure attachments. This progression is designed to deepen your understanding of how effective communication acts as a cornerstone for developing and maintaining healthy, secure relationships. As you continue to refine these skills, you'll be better equipped to create a network of support that is both understanding and supportive, paving the way for more meaningful and enduring connections.

UNLOCK THE POWER OF GENEROSITY

"The best way to find yourself is to lose yourself in the service of others." - *Mahatma Gandhi*

Helping others brings a special kind of happiness that can't be measured. Let's create a positive impact together!

Imagine someone like you—curious about *Anxious Attachment* but unsure if it's the right fit. Your thoughts and experiences could guide them on their journey.

I aim to make *the Anxious Attachment Recovery Solution* easy and accessible for everyone who seeks to build secure and lasting relationships.

But I can't do it alone. I need your help to reach more people who could benefit from this book.

Most people decide on a book based on what others have said about it. That's why I'm asking you to take a moment to share your thoughts. It won't cost you anything and will take just a minute, but it could make a difference in someone's life.

Your review could help...

...one more person overcome their fear of abandonment. ...one more reader find emotional stability.

...one more individual build lasting, secure relationships. ...one more person boost their self-esteem.

...one more reader heal from past trauma.

. . .

To make a difference, simply click on the QR code below and please leave a review:

If you love helping others, you're the kind of person I want on this journey.

Thank you from the bottom of my heart!

Luzivette Martinez, RN

5

FOSTERING SECURE ATTACHMENTS

I magine walking into a room where every glance and every interaction feels safe, understood, and valued. This sense of security doesn't stem from mere acquaintance but from deeply rooted emotional connections. This chapter delves into fostering such secure attachments not just as an ideal but as a tangible, achievable reality. Over my three decades as a registered nurse, I've witnessed countless individuals transform their relational dynamics from fear driven to secure, and the essence of this transformation lies in under standing and cultivating secure attachments.

UNDERSTANDING THE HALLMARKS OF SECURE ATTACHMENT

Define Secure Attachment

Secure attachment is the gold standard towards which many in the realm of psychological and relational health aspire. It is characterized by several key elements: emotional availability, mutual respect, and a balanced need for closeness and independence. Emotional availability involves being present and responsive to a partner's emotional needs, demonstrating empathy and understanding. Mutual respect refers to honoring each other's autonomy and values without imposing one's own needs unduly. Lastly, a balanced approach to closeness and independence means nurturing a relationship where both individuals feel free to pursue their personal growth while remaining interconnected. These traits foster a relationship environment where both parties feel secure enough to be vulnerable and strong in equal measure.

Contrast with Anxious Attachment

To appreciate the stability that secure attachment offers, it's useful to understand its contrast with anxious attachment. Where secure attachment is marked by tranquility and trust, anxious attachment often operates out of fear and uncertainty. Anxiously attached individuals may experience a constant need for reassurance, fear of abandonment, and difficulty trusting their partners' commitment. These feelings stem from deeply ingrained patterns often established in early life, where the unpredictability of emotional support leads to a hyper-vigilant attitude towards relational cues. In moments of stress, while securely attached individuals tend to seek and provide support effectively, those with anxious attachments might react with panic and insecurity, potentially escalating the stress and misunderstanding in the relationship.

Benefits of Secure Attachment

The benefits of developing a secure attachment style extend well into various dimensions of life. Relationally, secure attachments are associated with higher satisfaction and stability. Partners feel more connected and supportive, navigating life's challenges with greater resilience and cooperation. Conflict resolution becomes less about winning or losing and more about understanding and growth as both parties communicate openly without fear of judgment or rejection. These dynamics cultivate a deep seated sense of belonging and acceptance between partners, crucial for long-term relational health.

Impact on Overall Well-being

Beyond interpersonal relationships, secure attachment significantly enhances overall mental health and life satisfaction. Individuals with secure attachments generally exhibit lower anxiety and depression rates, as the stability in their relationships provides a strong buffer against stress. They are also likely to possess higher self-esteem and more robust emotional regulation skills, which contribute to a more positive outlook on life. This emotional stability allows them to tackle personal and professional challenges more effectively, leading to a more fulfilling and productive life. The ripple effects of secure attachments thus reinforce the notion that our relational health is intricately linked to our overall psychological and emotional well-being.

Fostering secure attachments enriches our relationships and enhances our individual capacity for joy, resilience, and emotional fulfillment. As we explore this chapter further, the focus will shift to practical strategies and insights aimed at nurturing these secure bonds in our relationships, paving the way for a healthier, more connected life.

STEPS TO TRANSITION FROM ANXIOUS TO SECURE ATTACHMENT

Transitioning from an anxious attachment style to a secure one often requires a reflective and proactive approach, where personal triggers are identified, self-soothing techniques are developed, and gradual changes are implemented within one's behavior and mindset. Let's explore how you can embark on this transformative path, which, while challenging, is immensely rewarding.

Identifying Personal Triggers

The first step in moving towards secure attachment involves a deep dive into understanding what specifically triggers your anxious reactions. These triggers are personal and can vary widely, but they often involve situations that subconsciously remind you of past insecurities or fears. An effective way to identify these triggers is through intro-spective exercises that encourage you to reflect on moments when you felt most anxious. Keeping a detailed journal can be particularly helpful here. In this journal, note situations, interactions, and even specific times of day when anxious feelings tend to arise. Look for patterns or common themes. For instance, you might notice that your anxiety peaks during periods of uncertainty in your relationship, such as waiting for a response to a message or when your partner is vague about their plans. Understanding these triggers is crucial, as it arms you with the knowledge to anticipate and manage your reac-tions better, setting the stage for more secure interactions.

Developing Self-soothing Techniques

Once you are aware of your triggers, the next step is to develop methods to calm yourself when anxiety strikes. Techniques such as mindfulness, positive self talk, and grounding exercises can be very effective. Mindfulness encourages you to stay present and focused rather than spiraling into worry about what might happen. It can be practiced through simple breathing exercises or through more struc-tured activities like mindfulness meditation. Positive self-talk involves changing the narrative in your head from one of fear and doubt to one of assurance and positivity. For example, replace thoughts like "They're not texting back because they're losing interest in me" with "They're likely busy at the moment; they care about me and will get back when they can." Grounding exercises help divert your focus from anxiety to the physical world around you. Techniques include tactile methods like holding a piece of ice, which focuses your mind on the intense cold sensation, thereby pulling your thoughts away from anxiety triggers.

Encouraging Gradual Change

Building secure attachment is a gradual process that involves making small, manageable changes over time. Start by setting small, realistic goals that aim to adjust your attachment behaviors. If you tend to seek constant reassurance from a partner, you might set a goal to refrain from asking for reassurance more than once during a conversation. Or, if you struggle with jealousy, you might work on trusting your partner's words rather than acting on unfounded fears. Each small victory in these behaviors will build your confidence and encourage further progress. It's also helpful to communicate openly with your partner about your goals and progress. This not only helps them understand your needs and changes, but also allows them to support you throughout your transition.

Seeking Therapeutic Support

Finally, consider seeking professional help to guide your transition to secure attachment. Therapies like cognitive-behavioral therapy (CBT) and attachment based therapy provide structured approaches to understanding and changing your attachment style. A therapist specializing in attachment issues can offer insights into your behaviors and patterns that you might not realize on your own. They can also provide personalized strategies and support as you work through the challenges of altering deep seated attachment behaviors. Remember, seeking help is a sign of strength and commitment to your wellbeing and the health of your relationships.

Incorporating these steps into your life does not mean that changes will happen overnight, but each step is a building block toward a more secure and fulfilling relationship. As you continue to work on identifying triggers, practicing self-soothing, making gradual changes, and possibly engaging with a therapist, you'll likely find that your reactions to relationship stressors become more balanced and less fear driven. This shift is crucial not just for your relationship health but for your overall emotional and mental wellbeing.

THE IMPORTANCE OF CONSISTENCY AND RELIABILITY

In the landscape of relationships, particularly for those navigating the challenges of anxious attachment, the concepts of consistency and reliability emerge as cornerstones for building secure, stable connections. When you can predict how your significant other will respond to your needs and emotions, a profound sense of safety and trust begins to flourish. This predictability is not about monotony or lack of spontaneity but rather about the assurance that the foundational elements of your relationship are steadfast and dependable.

Consistency in relationships means showing up, both physically and emotionally, in a way that is steady and predictable. It involves patterns of interaction that you and your partner can count on day after day, which is especially soothing for those who have experienced relational turbulence in the past. For someone with an anxious attachment style, unpredictable fluctuations in a partner's behavior can trigger deep seated fears of abandonment or rejection. Therefore, establishing a rhythm of predictability can significantly alleviate these fears. For instance, if you commit to regular check-ins with your partner at specific times of the day, it creates a routine that can help stabilize the relationship. These check-ins do not need to be lengthy or profound but should convey availability and attentiveness.

Reliability builds on the foundation of consistency. It extends beyond being emotionally available to fulfilling promises and commitments. When you say you will do something, whether it's something as simple as washing the dishes or as significant as attending a family event, following through on these commitments is crucial. This reliability reinforces trust and signals to your partner that they are a priority in your life, their needs and expectations are respected, and they can depend on you. This trust, cultivated through countless small acts of reliability, forms the bedrock upon which secure attachments are built.

Moreover, managing expectations plays a pivotal role in maintaining consistency and reliability. It involves openly discussing what you and your partner expect from each other and the relationship. These discussions can help clarify misunderstandings and set realistic standards for both partners. For example, if you have a demanding job that requires occasional late night work, communicating this clearly to your partner helps set the expectation that you might not always be available for evening plans. By managing these expectations, you reduce the likelihood of disappointments and misunderstandings, which are often triggers for anxiety in those with insecure attachment styles.

To further enhance the alignment between your actions and intentions, setting up feedback mechanisms can be amazingly beneficial. These mechanisms allow for regular, constructive conversations about how each partner feels the relationship is progressing. For example, you might establish a monthly "relationship check-in" where you both discuss what is going well and what might need adjustment. These check-ins can help ensure that both partners feel heard and valued and that any actions taken are in line with the mutually agreed upon expectations and values of the relationship. They provide a structured way to give and receive feedback, fostering an environment of open communication and continuous improvement.

Through these practices, consistency and reliability become more than just concepts they evolve into actionable, observable behaviors that significantly enhance relationship security. As you integrate these strategies into your relationship, you're likely to notice a shift towards greater stability and satisfaction, both of which are key indicators of a secure attachment forming. In essence, by embedding consistency and reliability into your daily interactions, you soothe your anxious attachment tendencies and pave the way for a relationship rich in trust and mutual respect. This shift is crucial for anyone looking to transform their relational dynamics from insecurity and unpredictability to a secure, loving partnership.

BUILDING TRUST: CORE PRINCIPLES AND PRACTICES

Trust is the bedrock upon which secure attachments are built. It forms the foundation that supports not only romantic relationships but also friendships and familial bonds. Building trust is a gradual process that involves consistent actions over time, where each inter-action serves as a brick in the edifice of your relational stability. When trust exists, individuals feel safe to express their thoughts and emotions, secure in the knowledge that they will be met with under-standing and respect. However, developing this trust requires more than just a passive presence; it necessitates intentional actions and decisions that demonstrate reliability, honesty, and commitment.

One critical aspect of building trust is transparency. This means being open about one's feelings, intentions, and concerns. It involves sharing your thoughts openly and honestly, even when it might be uncomfortable. Transparency fosters an environment where both parties feel understood and valued, significantly reducing the chances of misunderstandings and resentment. For instance, if you are feeling overwhelmed by work and need some space, openly communicating this to your partner prevents them from feeling neglected and builds trust by clarifying your actions. Similarly, accountability is vital in building trust. It requires owning up to your mistakes and making efforts to amend them. When you hold yourself accountable, you show your partner that you are committed to the health of the relationship and respect their feelings, which strengthens trust.

Rebuilding trust in relationships where it has been damaged is a deli-cate and often challenging process, but not impossible. The key to rebuilding trust lies in consistent and persistent efforts to change behaviors that broke the trust in the first place. For example, if infi-delity or deceit has damaged trust, the rebuilding process might involve open discussions about the factors that led to those actions and setting concrete steps to ensure they do not recur. Couples therapy can be exceptionally beneficial during this time, providing a structured environment to address issues and heal. Transparency, ongoing accountability, and gradual steps through consistent positive interactions are crucial in mending the broken trust. Each positive action, each commitment kept, and each honest conversation is a step towards healing and strengthening the relationship.

To further cement trust in relationships, engaging in trust-building exercises can be profoundly effective. These exercises are designed to enhance reliability, teamwork, and understanding. A simple but powerful exercise is the trust fall, where one partner relies on the other to catch them without looking. This exercise, although basic, can profoundly impact trust, as it involves physical and emotional vulnerability. Similarly, undertaking projects or activities that require collaboration and reliance on each other can strengthen trust. For instance, setting up a DIY home project, planning a trip together, or participating in a cooking class can create shared experiences that build teamwork and dependability, reinforcing the trust between you and your partner.

However, as you work on building or rebuilding trust, it's crucial to be mindful of common pitfalls that can undermine your efforts. Inconsistency is one of the major trust-destroyers in relationships. If your words do not match your actions, or if you are unreliable, it can quickly erode any trust you have built. Dishonesty, no matter how small it may seem, can also be significantly detrimental. Even small lies can lead to doubts about trustworthiness in more important matters. Lastly, failing to respect boundaries can severely impact trust. It is essential to understand and honor the limits each person sets in a relationship. Ignoring these boundaries disrespects your partner's needs and can lead to feelings of betrayal and mistrust.

Building trust is not about grand gestures but the small, consistent actions that show you are reliable, honest, and committed. Whether you are laying the foundation of trust in a new relationship, strengthening it in an existing one, or attempting to rebuild trust after a breach, the principles of transparency, accountability, and consistency remain key. By committing to these principles and actively engaging in practices that demonstrate your trustworthiness, you cultivate a relationship where both partners feel secure, valued, and connected. This trust becomes the cornerstone of not just surviving but thriving in your relationships, allowing both individuals to grow together in a supportive and understanding environment.

AVAILABLE PARTNERS

One of the most critical factors in fostering a secure and fulfilling relationship is your partner's emotional availability. Emotional availability refers to a person's ability to share their feelings openly, understand and respond to the emotions of others, and engage in a meaningful emotional exchange. It forms the backbone of a deep, resilient connection, enabling both partners to feel supported and understood. Recognizing the signs of emotional availability in potential partners can significantly increase your chances of developing a healthy, long-lasting relationship.

The signs of emotional availability are often evident in how someone communicates and reacts in various situations. Active listening is a key indicator. When a partner listens actively, they are not only hearing your words but are also engaged with and responsive to the underlying emotions. They may paraphrase what you've said, ask relevant questions, or provide feedback that indicates they understand your perspective. Responsiveness to emotional cues is another sign. An emotionally available partner can perceive and react appropriately to how you're feeling, whether you're joyful, stressed, or sad, providing comfort or sharing in your happiness in ways that are attuned to your emotional state. Lastly, openness about personal feelings is crucial. An emotionally available person will share their thoughts and feelings with honesty and vulnerability, trusting you with their inner emotional world. This openness fosters a deep mutual understanding and strengthens the bond between you.

The impact of having an emotionally available partner is profound. Such relationships are typically marked by greater satisfaction and stability. Knowing that you can rely on your partner to understand and empathize with your feelings creates a strong foundation of trust. This trust enables both partners to navigate conflicts more effectively, as each understands the other's perspective better and can address issues from a place of compassion and respect. Furthermore, emotional availability supports personal growth as both partners feel safe to explore their feelings and behaviors, learning from each other and evolving together. This dynamic leads to a more vibrant and enriching relationship where both individuals feel valued and supported.

Attracting emotionally available partners often begins with cultivating your own emotional availability. Reflect on how open you are with your feelings and how you respond to the emotions of others. Improving your emotional expressiveness and listening skills can make you more approachable and attractive to similarly emotionally available individuals. Practices like mindfulness and emotional regulation can enhance your awareness of your own emotions and how you react to others, making it easier for you to connect on a deeper emotional level. Furthermore, setting an example of emotional openness encourages reciprocity, creating a virtuous cycle of emotional sharing and connection.

However, it's equally important to be aware of the red flags of emotional unavailability, which can save you from potential heartache and frustration. These signs include a lack of communication about feelings, indirect behavior when topics of emotional significance are brought up, and a pattern of relationships where emotional depth is lacking. Other warning signs might include expressing discomfort with your emotions, a preference for superficial interactions, or a history of short relationships. Recognizing these signs early can help you make informed decisions about whether to pursue or continue a relationship, potentially saving you from investing in a partnership where emotional connection and support are limited.

In sum, understanding and recognizing emotional availability in others and yourself plays a pivotal role in forming and maintaining secure, satisfying relationships. By valuing and practicing emotional openness, responsiveness, and active listening, you set the stage for a relationship characterized by mutual understanding, respect, and deep emotional connection. This approach enriches your romantic relationships and enhances your interactions with friends and family, creating a broader environment of emotional support and satisfaction. As you continue to engage with these practices, remember that emotional availability is both a journey and a choiceone that leads to richer, more meaningful connections.

CULTIVATING EMPATHY AND UNDERSTANDING IN RELATIONSHIPS

Empathy, the ability to understand and share the feelings of another, stands as a cornerstone in the foundation of healthy and secure relationships. It goes beyond mere sympathy to actively engaging in the emotional experiences of others, making it a critical tool for deepening connections and enhancing communication. When you empathize, you not only hear what your partner is saying but also why they might be saying it and how it affects them emotionally. This profound level of understanding can transform interactions, turning potential conflicts into moments of bonding and mutual respect.

To effectively cultivate empathy, you can start by practicing reflective listening. This technique involves listening to your partner's words and then reflecting back on what you've heard, not just in terms of content but also feeling. For example, if your partner expresses frustration over a busy work schedule, you might respond with, "It sounds like you're really overwhelmed and stressed with your workload." This response shows that you're listening and engaging with their emotional state. Reflective listening validates your partner's feelings and encourages a more open and honest dialogue where both partners feel heard and understood.

Another powerful technique for developing empathy is perspective taking. This involves actively trying to see the world through your partner's eyes and understanding their reactions from their viewpoint. It requires a temporary suspension of your beliefs and assumptions to fully appreciate their experiences and emotions. Engaging in perspective taking can be particularly useful in resolving conflicts, as it allows you to understand the motivations behind your partner's actions or words, which might not be apparent from your viewpoint. By regularly practicing this, you can foster a deeper emotional connection and reduce misunderstandings, as both partners feel their perspectives are considered and valued.

Empathy mapping, a tool from user experience design, can enhance understanding and communication in relationships by visually mapping what your partner might be seeing, thinking, feeling, and doing in a situation. This helps you step into their shoes and better understand their emotional world. If your partner seems upset when you mention going out with friends, empathy mapping can reveal underlying reasons. They might feel neglected, thinking you prioritize others over them, leading to emotions like loneliness or insecurity. As a result, they might withdraw or become irritable. Recognizing this can prompt a more compassionate response, like discussing how to balance social life with quality time together. Collaborative Empathy Mapping, creating empathy maps together can deepen understanding and communication. By exploring each other's triggers and needs, you can develop strategies to address concerns and strengthen your connection.

The role of empathy in conflict resolution cannot be overstated. Empathy allows you to understand your partner's feelings and viewpoints, helping deescalate potential conflicts before they become heated arguments. When both partners practice empathy, they approach conflicts not as adversaries but as allies who are trying to solve a problem together. This approach not only makes it easier to find mutually satisfying solutions but also strengthens the relationship by reinforcing a pattern of respectful, supportive interaction, even in the face of disagreement.

Creating a culture of empathy within a relationship means consistently choosing to engage with your partner's emotions, striving to understand their perspective, and communicating your understanding. This culture encourages an environment where both partners feel safe expressing their true thoughts and feelings, knowing they will be met with understanding and not judgment. This emotional safety is crucial for fostering longterm relational stability and satisfaction, as it builds a foundation of trust and openness that supports both individual growth and collective harmony.

To cultivate such a culture, make empathy a regular practice rather than a response to conflict. Incorporate empathic communication into daily interactions, take time to engage in perspective taking exercises and create opportunities for emotional sharing that build understanding and closeness. By making empathy a cornerstone of your relationship, you nurture a connection that is not only resilient in the face of challenges but also rich with emotional depth and mutual respect.

As this chapter closes, remember that fostering secure attachments through empathy is not merely about avoiding conflict or smoothing over differences. It is about building a profound understanding and connection that enhances every interaction with your partner, creating an emotionally rich, deeply satisfying relationship. In the next chapter, we will explore practical tools and strategies that can further strengthen your relationships, providing you with the skills and knowledge to build lasting bonds based on mutual respect, understanding, and love.

6

PRACTICAL TOOLS FOR LASTING CHANGE

I magine starting each day not just with the chime of an alarm but with a personal ritual that grounds you, centers your emotions, and prepares you for the relational dynamics of the day. In this chapter, we delve into the art and science of crafting daily routines that nurture your attachment health, ensuring that each day contributes positively to your journey toward secure relationships. Here, the focus shifts from understanding and healing to actively cultivating an environment—both internally and externally—that fosters emotional resilience and secure attachment.

DAILY ROUTINES FOR ATTACHMENT HEALTH

Establish Morning Rituals

The way you start your morning can set the tone for your entire day, particularly when it comes to your emotional and relational health. Integrating positive affirmations into your morning routine can be a transformative practice. These affirmations should focus on security and self-worth, directly countering the insecurities that often plague those with anxious attachment styles. Phrases like "I am worthy of love and respect" or "I am secure within myself" can fortify your self-esteem and prepare you emotionally to face the day's challenges.

Incorporating a brief mindfulness exercise each morning further enhances your ability to remain centered throughout the day. Just five minutes of mindfulness meditation can help you cultivate a state of calm awareness, reducing reactivity to the day's stresses. This practice trains your mind to remain present and engaged, helping you navigate relational dynamics more effectively.

Keeping a gratitude journal each morning also contributes to this foundation. By documenting things, you are grateful for, you shift your focus from fears and insecurities to positivity and appreciation. This shift improves your mood and broadens your perspective, helping you appreciate your relationships and the progress you are making in healing your attachment issues.

Integrate Attachment-Focused Activities

Throughout the day, intentional check-ins with loved ones can significantly reinforce your sense of security and belonging. These check-ins—whether a brief text message, a phone call, or a lunch date—are not about seeking reassurance but about nurturing the connection. For those working through anxious attachment, regular, meaningful interaction with loved ones provides practical affirmation of the security and stability of these relationships.

Scheduled self-reflection is another critical daily activity. Taking time to reflect on your interactions and feelings each day allows you to process your experiences consciously. This practice can help you identify triggers and patterns in your attachment behavior, providing insights that are crucial for continued personal growth. Whether it's a midday review or an evening reflection, this practice encourages ongoing self-awareness and mindful engagement with your emotional health.

. . .

Promote Consistent Bedtime Routines

A calming bedtime routine is essential for closing your day with the same intentionality with which you started. This routine might include reading something uplifting, reflecting on the day's positive interactions, or engaging in a brief meditation session. These activities help you unwind and reinforce a positive, calm mental state, reducing anxiety and promoting better sleep. Good sleep is crucial for emotional regulation and resilience, directly impacting your ability to maintain secure attachments.

Encourage Regular Physical Activity

Regular physical exercise is a potent tool for mood regulation and stress reduction. Activities like walking, yoga, or team sports do not just keep you physically healthy but also enhance your emotional equilibrium. Exercise releases endorphins, known as 'feel-good' hormones, which can elevate your mood and reduce feelings of anxiety and depression. For those with anxious attachment, regular exercise provides a dual benefit: it improves physical health while also contributing to emotional stability, making it easier to maintain healthy relationships.

By embedding these practices into your daily routine, you create a structured approach to nurturing your emotional health and cultivating secure attachments. Each element of your routine builds on the others, creating a comprehensive strategy for strengthening your resilience and transforming your relational dynamics. This intentional approach to daily life ensures that every day is a step forward in your path toward lasting change and secure relationships.

Journaling for Emotional Clarity and Insight

Imagine a tool so powerful that it can help you untangle the web of your emotions, clarify your thoughts, and track your personal growth over time. This tool is journaling, a practice that has been used for centuries as a means of self-exploration and expression. For those dealing with anxious attachment, journaling can be particularly beneficial as it provides a safe, private space to process emotions, understand attachment behaviors, and observe changes over time. By putting pen to paper, you create a personal space to express your thoughts and feelings without judgment, allowing you to gain more in-depth insights into your own emotional patterns and triggers.

Journaling acts like a mirror, reflecting your inner world back to you. When you write about your experiences and emotions, you are essentially telling your story, and in doing so, you begin to see patterns and themes that recur in your life. This reflective practice can be especially enlightening for those with anxious attachment, as it can reveal the specific situations or interactions that trigger feelings of insecurity or fear. For instance, journaling about times when you felt abandoned or overly clingy can help you identify the circumstances or behaviors that precipitated these feelings. Over time, this awareness can empower you to manage your reactions and approach relationships with more confidence and less fear.

To enhance the benefits of journaling, it is helpful to use structured prompts that focus specifically on your attachment issues. Prompts such as "Today, I felt secure when..." or "I felt anxious today because..." guide your reflection, making it easier to connect your daily experiences with your broader attachment patterns. These prompts encourage you to explore both the positive and challenging aspects of your day, which can help you recognize and celebrate your progress, as well as identify areas where you might need further growth. As you respond to these prompts over time, you'll start to compile a detailed record of your emotional landscape, which can be an invaluable resource in your healing process.

Reflecting on your journal entries is a critical aspect of this practice. This isn't about rereading your entries for the sake of nostalgia; rather, it's about analyzing them to understand your emotional triggers and patterns. After journaling for a few weeks, take some time to go back and review your entries. Look for patterns in your behavior or emotional reactions that may be linked to your anxious attachment. For example, you might notice that your anxiety peaks during periods of transition or uncertainty or that certain types of interactions consistently make you feel insecure. Recognizing these patterns is the first step toward changing them. It allows you to anticipate and prepare for situations that might challenge your emotional stability, helping you develop healthier responses and, over time, begin to form more secure attachments.

To keep this practice useful and relevant, it's important to review your journal entries periodically. This regular review helps you track your progress and keeps you engaged with your personal growth journey. Set a reminder to review your entries every month or at another regular interval that works for you. During these reviews, celebrate your progress, reflect on recurring challenges, and adjust your coping strategies as needed. This ongoing process maintains your motivation and deepens your understanding of your attachment style and how it affects your relationships.

Through journaling, you have a unique opportunity to witness your own evolution in real time. This practice offers more than just a record of days; it provides insights into your emotional growth and resilience. As you continue to journal, you'll find that this simple tool helps you manage your anxious attachment and supports your overall well-being, paving the way for more secure and satisfying relationships.

USING TECHNOLOGY FOR ATTACHMENT HEALING: APPS AND ONLINE RESOURCES

In the digital age, technology offers unprecedented tools for personal growth and emotional healing, particularly for those navigating the complexities of attachment issues. The right apps and online resources can serve as valuable allies on your path to overcoming insecurity and fear of abandonment, complementing traditional therapeutic methods and daily practices. Here, you'll discover a curated list of digital tools specifically designed to support mental health and attachment healing. These resources have been carefully selected to empower you with practical tools that can enhance your understanding and management of anxious attachment.

Recommend Relevant Apps

Among the myriad of apps available, mindfulness apps like "Headspace" and "Calm" stand out for their utility in fostering a state of mental calmness and presence, which is crucial for those dealing with anxious attachment. These apps offer guided meditation sessions that can help reduce anxiety, a common symptom of insecure attachment, by teaching you how to focus on the present moment and reduce ruminative thinking patterns. Mood trackers such as "Daylio" allow you to monitor your emotional states, helping you to identify triggers and patterns in your mood fluctuations. This can be particularly enlightening for understanding the situations or interactions that exacerbate your attachment anxieties. Furthermore, therapy apps like "Talkspace" and "BetterHelp" provide access to professional counseling services from the comfort of your home, making psychological support more accessible than ever. These platforms connect you with licensed therapists who can offer guidance tailored to your specific attachment concerns, facilitating progress even outside traditional therapy sessions.

Guide to Online Courses

For those who are motivated by structured learning, various reputable online platforms offer courses on attachment theory, emotional regulation, and relationship building. Websites like Coursera and Udemy feature courses taught by qualified professionals in psychology and counseling. For instance, a course on "Attachment Theory for Personal Growth" can provide you with a more in-depth understanding of how your early childhood experiences have shaped your attachment style and offer strategies for developing more secure attachment patterns. Similarly, courses on emotional regulation can teach you practical skills to manage anxiety and emotional reactivity, both of which are crucial for those struggling with fear of abandonment. Engaging in these courses broadens your knowledge and equips you with practical tools to apply in your everyday life, enhancing your journey toward secure relationships.

Encourage Participation in Online Forums

Participation in online forums and social media groups can be amazingly beneficial, especially for those who might feel isolated in their struggles with attachment issues. Platforms like Reddit and Facebook host numerous groups where individuals share their experiences, challenges, and successes related to attachment and mental health. For example, joining a group dedicated to discussing anxious attachment can provide you with insights from others who face similar challenges, offering new perspectives and coping strategies. These forums also allow you to share your own experiences, which can be cathartic and affirming. The sense of community and understanding you gain from interacting with others who empathize with your situation can be a powerful antidote to the loneliness and misunderstanding that often accompany attachment issues.

Advice on Digital Balance

While the benefits of digital resources are manifold, it's crucial to maintain a healthy balance between the online and offline worlds. Excessive reliance on digital tools can lead to a disconnection from face-to-face interactions and real-world relationships, which are essential for building and maintaining secure attachments. It's important to use these tools as supplements rather than replacements for direct human contact. Make a conscious effort to engage in real-life interactions with friends, family, and peers, which provide irreplaceable emotional support and connection. Additionally, set boundaries around your digital consumption to prevent information overload and ensure that your technology use supports rather than hinders your emotional and relational goals.

By integrating these digital tools and resources into your healing process, you can enhance your capacity to manage anxious attachment and build healthier relationships. Each app, course, and forum offers unique benefits that can support you in different aspects of your journey, providing flexibility and accessibility in how you choose to engage with your personal growth. As you navigate these resources, remember that each step taken with these tools brings you closer to a more in-depth understanding of yourself and a more secure foundation in your relationships.

Group Therapy and Support Networks

Engaging in group therapy and cultivating support networks are critical avenues for those seeking to overcome insecure attachments and foster healthier, more fulfilling relationships. Group therapy, in particular, offers a structured environment where individuals can explore their attachment issues safely under the guidance of a professional. This setting provides a unique opportunity to gain multiple perspectives on common issues, allowing participants to see their experiences reflected in others, which can significantly reduce feelings of isolation and stigma. Within these sessions, you can share your thoughts and feelings, receive feedback, and engage in therapeutic exercises designed to promote understanding and healing. The collective experience of group therapy often leads to profound insights and fosters a sense of communal healing that can be difficult to achieve in one-on-one settings.

The benefits of group therapy extend beyond individual insights. As you listen to others share their struggles and successes, you gain diverse perspectives that can challenge and refine your own understanding of attachment. This exposure to multiple viewpoints can also inspire new strategies for managing your fears and insecurities, providing a broader toolkit for handling relationship challenges. Moreover, group therapy sessions are often a source of real-time support. Seeing others actively working through similar issues can be amazingly motivating, reinforcing your own commitment to the healing process. This environment also allows for the development of empathy, as you recognize the struggles of others and offer support, which, in return, can make you feel more connected and supported.

In addition to formal therapy groups, joining or forming less structured support networks can also play a vital role in your healing journey. These networks could be in-person groups, such as local meetups or interest-based clubs, or virtual communities that connect individuals from various backgrounds. The key is to engage with groups that emphasize positivity, growth, and emotional support. Whether these are book clubs, hiking groups, or online forums focused on mental health, the interaction and mutual support provided can significantly enhance your sense of belonging and emotional well-being.

When choosing a group, whether for therapy or more informal support, several factors should be considered to ensure it aligns with your needs and goals. Confidentiality is paramount; a safe space where personal experiences can be shared without fear of judgment or exposure is crucial for effective therapy and support. Additionally, the group should have a clear structure and focus, whether on personal growth, specific types of therapy, or shared activities that foster connection. The facilitator's qualifications and approach are also important, especially in therapeutic settings, as they should be skilled in guiding discussions and managing group dynamics in a way that benefits all participants. Lastly, consider the overall atmosphere of the group. It should be one of encouragement and respect, where all members feel valued and able to contribute.

Personal stories and anecdotes further illustrate the transformative impact of group therapy and support networks. Consider the story of Elena, a young graphic designer who struggled with severe anxiety due to her anxious attachment style. Feeling isolated in her fears, she joined a group therapy session for individuals dealing with similar issues. Over several months, Elena found not only did her understanding of her attachment style deepen through discussions and shared experiences, but she also developed significant friendships within the group. These new connections provided her with a practical support system that helped her navigate her anxieties in healthier ways. Elena's experience highlights how group therapy can serve as a powerful catalyst for personal growth and the building of supportive relationships that extend beyond the therapy sessions.

By actively participating in group therapy and support networks, you are taking important steps toward understanding and managing your attachment style and building a community of support that can enhance your journey toward secure and fulfilling relationships. These communal experiences enrich your healing process, providing both the insights and the emotional support necessary to foster lasting change.

Preventing Relapse: Signs and Solutions

Navigating the complex terrain of emotional health, especially when overcoming insecure attachment patterns, is akin to maintaining a delicate balance. You've made significant strides, embraced new coping mechanisms, and perhaps felt more secure in your relationships than ever before. However, it's natural in any process of significant change to face moments where old habits resurface. Recognizing these early signs of a potential relapse into insecure attachment behaviors is crucial. It's like noticing storm clouds gathering after enjoying days of clear skies—you know it's time to take protective measures.

For someone working through attachment issues, increased anxiety or reverting to old coping mechanisms such as excessive reassurance-seeking or distancing oneself from loved ones can signal a slide back into old patterns. These signs are your psyche's indicators that underlying fears or unresolved issues are being triggered. The key here is not to panic but to recognize these signs early and address them proactively. For instance, if you find yourself obsessively checking your phone for messages from a partner, it might be a cue that your anxiety is spiking and old fears are at play.

Creating a personal relapse prevention plan is akin to drafting a personalized roadmap that guides you back to emotional stability whenever you find yourself veering off. This plan involves identifying strategies that have worked for you in the past and setting up a system to implement them quickly when signs of relapse appear. Maybe you've found that reaching out to a therapist or a trusted friend helps you regain perspective when you're feeling insecure. Or perhaps revisiting journal entries where you've recorded your growth and the strategies that helped can remind you of the progress you've made and the tools at your disposal. Including self-soothing practices such as deep breathing exercises, mindfulness, or engaging in a hobby that centers you can also be part of this plan. The idea is to have a clear set of actionable steps that you can turn to, which reduces panic and gives you a sense of control.

Communication plays a pivotal role in maintaining the gains you've made in your emotional health. It's essential to cultivate an environment where you can openly discuss your struggles without fear of judgment. This means having at least one or two people in your life with whom you can share your feelings openly and who can offer support and accountability. These individuals act as your emotional touchstones, helping you navigate moments of doubt and reinforcing your commitment to your growth. Whether it's a friend, family member, therapist, or support group, these relationships are crucial in providing the encouragement and perspective needed during challenging times.

Self-compassion is perhaps the most critical element in dealing with potential relapses. It's easy to be hard on yourself when old patterns emerge, to feel as if you are failing or regressing. Embracing a compassionate view of yourself is vital. Understand that setbacks are part of the process and not indicators of failure. Each step back is an opportunity to learn more about yourself, to refine your strategies, and to deepen your resilience. Treat yourself with the same kindness and understanding that you would offer a good friend in distress. Remember, the path to secure attachment and emotional well-being is not linear but a series of advances and retreats, each providing valuable lessons. By maintaining self-compassion, you transform your setbacks into steps forward, continuing to build a foundation of secure, fulfilling relationships and a resilient sense of self.

In essence, preventing relapse into insecure attachment behaviors involves a blend of early recognition, proactive planning, supportive communication, and, fundamentally, a compassionate approach to self-growth. Each element plays a crucial role in navigating the ebbs and flows of your emotional development, ensuring that each challenge is met with effective strategies and a supportive network, fostering continued growth and stability in your journey toward lasting emotional well-being.

LONG-TERM GOALS FOR SECURE ATTACHMENT

Setting long-term goals for developing secure attachments transforms the abstract concept of emotional health into concrete, achievable targets. These goals act as guiding beacons on your path to healthier relationships and a more stable emotional life. Begin by defining what secure attachment looks like for you. Is it the ability to communicate openly with your partner? Or perhaps it's about feeling at ease when alone, without the nagging fear that solitude equates to loneliness. Once you pinpoint what secure attachment means in your context, you can start setting specific, realistic goals to achieve it.

For instance, improving communication in your relationships can be a tangible goal if you often find yourself misunderstood or if you tend to misinterpret others' intentions. A practical step towards this goal might be to learn and practice active listening skills. You could set a goal to engage in at least one meaningful conversation per day, where you focus entirely on understanding the other person's perspective without immediately crafting your response. Another goal might be to consistently practice self-care, which is crucial for anyone looking to heal from anxious attachment. This could mean scheduling regular times each week for activities that you find relaxing or rejuvenating, such as yoga, reading, or engaging in a hobby. Regularly attending therapy sessions is also a profound step towards understanding and mitigating the patterns that contribute to insecure attachment. By committing to ongoing professional guidance, you provide yourself with a structured environment for growth and learning.

Encouraging incremental progress is key to maintaining motivation and making your goals feel attainable. Break down each large goal into smaller, manageable milestones. If your goal is to enhance communication with your partner, start by identifying the specific aspects of communication you wish to improve, such as expressing your needs clearly or managing conflict more effectively. Then, set weekly or monthly objectives that bring you closer to these improvements. Celebrating these smaller victories not only boosts your morale but also reinforces your commitment to the overarching goal of secure attachment.

Regular evaluations of your progress are essential to ensure you remain on track and adjust your strategies as needed. Periodic assessments allow you to reflect on what's working and what isn't, providing an opportunity to realign your actions with your goals. This might involve journaling about your experiences and reviewing your entries to identify patterns and shifts in your behavior or scheduling regular check-ins with your therapist to discuss progress and setbacks. These evaluations can help you stay engaged with your goals and adapt your methods effectively, ensuring continual growth towards secure attachment.

Lifelong learning about attachment, relationships, and personal growth plays a crucial role in maintaining and enhancing your emotional health. Engage with books, workshops, and seminars that offer new insights into emotional well-being and relationship dynamics. This commitment to education keeps you informed about the latest research and theories in psychology and social behavior, enriching your understanding and application of healthy attachment practices. Whether it's through reading a new book on relationship psychology each month or attending a workshop on emotional regulation, each learning opportunity broadens your perspective and equips you with practical tools for strengthening your relationships.

By setting clear goals, celebrating incremental progress, regularly evaluating your journey, and committing to ongoing education, you create a robust framework for developing secure attachments. These practices enhance your relationships and contribute to a fuller, more satisfying emotional life. As you continue to invest in these areas, you solidify the foundations of security and trust in yourself and your relationships, paving the way for lasting emotional resilience and fulfillment.

In wrapping up this chapter on Practical Tools for Lasting Change, remember that the path to secure attachment is both rewarding and challenging. It requires consistency, patience, and a willingness to explore and address deep-seated emotions and patterns. By implementing the practices discussed, you are well on your way to forming healthier relationships and a more stable emotional environment. As we transition into the next chapter, we will build on these foundations, exploring advanced strategies for sustaining and deepening the secure attachments you have begun to develop.

7

CASE STUDIES AND SUCCESS TRUST

I magine a mosaic, each piece a story of transformation and triumph over anxious attachment. This chapter lays out a vivid tableau of individuals from varying backgrounds who have navigated the turbulent waters of insecurity and fear, ultimately anchoring themselves in the serene harbor of secure attachment. Each narrative not only serves as a testament to the universal potential for change but also illuminates the specific strategies and committed efforts that facilitated their remarkable transformations.

FROM ANXIOUS TO SECURE: REAL-LIFE TRANSFORMATIONS

Highlight Diverse Backgrounds

The journey from anxious to secure attachment is as diverse as humanity itself. Consider Elena, a young graphic designer from a bustling city whose early experiences were marked by abrupt parental separations—her parents frequently split up and reconciled, leaving her constantly unsure of who would be there for her. This instability fostered deep-seated fears of abandonment. Contrast her story with that of Raj, a middle-aged teacher from a small rural community who internalized intense fears of inadequacy after growing up in a highly critical household. Despite their different backgrounds, both found themselves bound by the chains of anxious attachment, profoundly impacting their relationships and self-esteem. However, their stories converge on a shared path of healing, illustrating that transformation is accessible to anyone, regardless of their past or present circumstances.

Detail Specific Strategies Used

Elena's breakthrough came from her dedication to mindfulness practices, which she integrated into her daily routine. These practices helped her cultivate a present-moment awareness that gradually reduced her pervasive anxiety about the future. She learned to ground herself in the reality of the now rather than getting lost in the "what ifs" of tomorrow. Raj, on the other hand, found solace and transformation in consistent therapy sessions. His therapist used a blend of cognitive-behavioral techniques to help him challenge and reframe the deeply ingrained belief of never being "enough." Raj was also introduced to self-help techniques, which were mainly focused on building self-compassion, which became a cornerstone of his practice towards securing his attachments.

Discuss Timeframe and Commitment

The timelines of Elena and Raj's transformations underscore a vital truth: profound change requires both time and commitment. Elena's journey towards secure attachment spanned over two years of daily mindfulness practices, coupled with regular participation in a support group for individuals struggling with similar issues. Raj's path involved three years of bi-weekly therapy sessions and daily engagement with self-help exercises. These stories highlight that while the path to secure attachment is not a quick fix, the investment of time and consistent effort is well worth the profound peace and improved relationships it brings.

Inspire with Positive Outcomes

Today, Elena and Raj enjoy the kind of secure, fulfilling relationships that once seemed beyond their reach. Elena reports not only greater stability in her romantic life but also enhanced connections with her family and friends, describing her relationships as deeply rooted in mutual trust and respect. Raj's transformation has significantly boosted his self-esteem and professional relationships, where he now feels confident to express his ideas and assert his needs. The positive outcomes in their personal and professional lives speak volumes about the power of transitioning from anxious to secure attachment, serving as a beacon of hope for anyone who finds themselves shackled by the fears of their inner child.

These narratives are more than just stories; they are real-life validations of the strategies discussed throughout this book. They serve as both inspiration and practical guides for you as you navigate your own path to secure attachment. As you reflect on these transformations, consider the steps that might resonate most with your situation. Whether it's adopting mindfulness like Elena or engaging in consistent therapeutic work like Raj, remember that your journey is unique, and what works for one may not work for another. The key is to persist, remain patient with yourself, and keep your eyes on the profound peace and relational stability that lie ahead.

OVERCOMING SETBACKS: LESSONS LEARNED

Navigating the path to secure attachment is seldom a linear process; it is punctuated with challenges and setbacks that can make even the most determined among us feel like relinquishing the fight. Yet, it is within these trials—turbulent relationships, personal crises, and unexpected life changes—that invaluable lessons and profound growth often occur. Recognizing the common hurdles and learning from those who have stumbled and stood up again can provide both solace and strategy for those still walking the path.

Setbacks such as enduring a breakup, facing rejection, or personal loss are not just obstacles; they are also opportunities to test and strengthen one's resilience and commitment to personal growth. These challenges often provoke a reevaluation of old patterns and can catalyze significant emotional and relational development. For instance, the end of a significant relationship, although painful, might also serve as a catalyst for an individual to reevaluate their needs and attachment patterns, leading to a more in-depth understanding of themselves and how they relate to others. This process of turning pain into insight requires a supportive environment—friends, family, therapists—who can provide both comfort and perspective during times of distress.

The role of support networks in navigating these setbacks cannot be overstated. Having a community or a skilled therapist provides not just an emotional cushion but also practical guidance and feedback. They can help identify the lessons embedded in each setback and assist in developing strategies to address them. For example, therapy can offer a space to explore the triggers that lead to insecure attachment behaviors and help develop healthier coping strategies. Support groups provide a sense of belonging and shared experience that can be profoundly reassuring. Knowing others have faced similar challenges and overcome them can be empowering.

Personal resilience also plays a crucial role. Self-care practices such as mindfulness, exercise, or journaling might bolster this resilience, maintaining one's mental health and providing the strength to face relational challenges. It is also nurtured by an attitude of openness to learning and growth, a willingness to question oneself, and to accept sometimes painful truths about one's behaviors and needs.

Every setback is a lesson to be learned, an opportunity for growth that, if seized, can significantly accelerate one's journey toward secure attachment. Each challenge faced and overcome reinforces the individual's resilience and deepens their understanding of themselves and their relational dynamics. This enhanced understanding is invaluable; it prevents future setbacks and enriches the person's capacity to form healthy, satisfying relationships that are built on a secure attachment foundation.

For you, the reader, who might be facing setbacks on your own path, let these stories be a reminder of the resilience of the human spirit and the transformative power of dedicated effort. Remember that each setback is not a detour off the path but a part of the path itself. It is through overcoming these challenges that we often find our greatest strengths and insights. So embrace these challenges, lean on your support network, engage with professional help if needed, and continue to invest in your resilience. Each step, each setback, and each recovery brings you closer to the secure, fulfilling relationships you seek.

THE ROLE OF PROFESSIONAL HELP IN ATTACHMENT RECOVERY

Navigating the terrain of anxious attachment often requires more than just willpower and self-help strategies; a structured, informed approach that professional therapy provides can be invaluable. In the realm of attachment recovery, various therapeutic approaches offer unique perspectives and tools that cater to the nuanced needs of individuals striving to transform their relational patterns. Among these, cognitive-behavioral therapy (CBT), psychodynamic therapy, and couples counseling stand out as beacons of hope, each offering distinct methodologies that address the roots and manifestations of anxious attachment.

CBT, a widely recognized approach, focuses on identifying and changing negative thought patterns that fuel anxieties and fears. It operates on the principle that our thoughts, feelings, and behaviors are interconnected and that by altering one component, we can influence the others. For someone grappling with anxious attachment, CBT provides practical tools to challenge and reframe the catastrophic thinking that often leads to an overwhelming fear of abandonment. This therapy equips you with skills to counteract the automatic negative thoughts that threaten your relationships, fostering a more balanced and less fear-driven perspective on interpersonal connections.

In contrast, psychodynamic therapy delves deeper into the emotional undercurrents that shape your attachment style. Rooted in the understanding that early childhood experiences significantly influence your adult relationships, this therapy focuses on uncovering and understanding these foundational experiences. By exploring your personal history, psychodynamic therapy helps you uncover patterns that have their genesis in your earliest interactions with caregivers. This insight is crucial, as it allows you to understand the "why" behind your emotional reactions, providing a clearer path to healing and change. The therapeutic relationship itself—characterized by trust, empathy, and unconditional support—serves as a corrective emotional experience, offering you a model of secure attachment that can be internalized and replicated in your external relationships.

Couples counseling, another pivotal therapeutic approach, addresses anxious attachment within the context of relationship dynamics. It provides a platform for both partners to explore how their attachment styles interact, often revealing patterns that exacerbate insecurity and fear. Through guided discussions and structured exercises, couples learn to communicate more effectively, articulate their needs clearly, and respond to each other's emotional cues with understanding and support. This cooperative approach not only alleviates symptoms of anxious attachment but also strengthens the relationship's foundation, making it a robust arena for mutual growth and healing.

The long-term benefits of engaging with professional help extend far beyond achieving a secure attachment. Individuals who undergo therapy often report improvements in various areas of their lives, including boosted self-esteem and enhanced stress management. These improvements are attributable to the increased emotional intelligence and resilience that therapy cultivates. As you learn to manage your attachment anxieties, you also acquire skills to handle other life stresses more effectively, leading to a more balanced and fulfilling life. This holistic enhancement of your well-being is a compelling reason to consider therapy not just as a remedy but as a transformative journey toward a more empowered self.

If you find yourself resonating with the struggles and aspirations mentioned, consider professional help as a viable and effective avenue for overcoming anxious attachment. Therapy can offer you the tools, understanding, and support needed to change not only how you relate to others but also how you see yourself. With professional guidance, the path to secure attachment and emotional fulfillment is not just a possibility but a tangible goal within your reach. Embrace this opportunity to redefine your relationships and reclaim your emotional autonomy, stepping into a life marked by deeper connections and genuine security.

COUPLES' THERAPY: REBUILDING ATTACHMENTS TOGETHER

In the intimate dance of a relationship, where two individuals come together to share their lives, the steps can sometimes become misaligned, particularly when the partners come from backgrounds of anxious or avoidant attachments. Couples' therapy serves as a choreographer of sorts, helping to realign these steps and restore harmony. This form of therapy is not just about resolving conflicts or addressing individual issues, but about enhancing the connection between partners and helping them develop a more secure attachment. The therapy process often involves a range of techniques designed to foster openness, understanding, and mutual support. One such technique is shared goal-setting, where the therapist helps the couple identify and articulate their common objectives for the relationship. These goals might pertain to communication, intimacy, or personal growth, and they serve as a roadmap for the therapy process, giving both partners a clear sense of direction and purpose.

Communication exercises are another cornerstone of couples' therapy, designed to enhance transparency and empathy within the relationship. These exercises might include practicing active listening, where one partner shares their thoughts or feelings while the other focuses solely on understanding and reflecting back on what is heard, without judgment or immediate reaction. This practice improves communication skills and deepens emotional connection, as partners feel heard and understood by each other. Another effective exercise is the expression of needs and boundaries, where partners learn to articulate their personal needs and limits clearly and respectfully. This open declaration helps prevent misunderstandings and builds a foundation of respect and care, essential components of a secure attachment.

The success stories of couples who have navigated the journey from insecure to secure attachments through therapy are both inspiring and enlightening. Take, for example, Lisa and Tom, a couple who entered therapy after years of recurrent conflicts and growing emotional distance. Both had come from families where emotional expression was discouraged, leading them to develop avoidant attachment styles. Through couples' therapy, they engaged in intensive communication exercises that helped them break down their walls of detachment and express their vulnerabilities. Over the course of a year, they learned to support each other's emotional needs, transforming their relationship into a source of strength and security.

As part of their therapeutic work, Lisa and Tom, like many other couples, underwent significant role adjustments within their relationship. Initially, Tom took on the role of the problem-solver, often dismissing emotions in favor of practical solutions, which left Lisa feeling misunderstood and isolated. Therapy helped them recognize and shift these dynamics. Tom learned to embrace his vulnerability and express his emotions more openly, while Lisa learned to assert her needs more directly. These role adjustments were crucial in breaking their cycle of miscommunication and emotional avoidance, paving the way for a more balanced and fulfilling relationship.

The mutual effort and commitment of both partners are critical to the success of couples' therapy. It requires both individuals to actively engage in the process, to be willing to explore their vulnerabilities, and to work on themselves, not just as partners but as individuals. This dual commitment enhances the effectiveness of the therapy and reinforces the bond between the partners, making their relationship a true partnership of growth and healing. The willingness to invest in this process, to endure the discomfort of growth, and to support each other through the challenges is what ultimately transforms an insecure attachment into a secure, resilient one.

In couples' therapy, the journey of each couple is unique and tailored to their specific histories, personalities, and dynamics. Yet, the underlying theme remains the same: fostering a secure, supportive, and understanding relationship where both partners feel valued and connected. This therapeutic process is not just about navigating past troubles but about building a future together, a future where both individuals feel secure not only in their relationship but in themselves. As couples evolve through therapy, they often discover not just a greater love for each other but a greater strength within themselves, a testament to the power of shared healing and mutual commitment.

SINGLE TO SECURE: STORIES OF PERSONAL EMPOWERMENT

In a society that often glorifies romantic partnerships as the hallmark of personal fulfillment, it's vital to illuminate the journeys of those who cultivate secure attachment from a place of singleness. For many, the period of being single is not just a time of waiting but a profound phase of personal development and self-discovery. This section celebrates individuals who have embraced their solo experiences to foster a sense of security and self-worth that is independent of romantic involvement.

Take, for instance, the story of Clara, a vibrant art curator who, after a series of tumultuous relationships, decided to focus solely on her personal growth. Clara's journey towards secure attachment began with a conscious decision to nurture her passions and interests, which had been neglected in her pursuit of romantic validation. She immersed herself in the art community, not just as a curator but as an artist herself, rediscovering her love for painting—a passion she had set aside since college. This reconnection with her creative self brought a profound sense of fulfillment and joy that no external relationship had offered. It was through this process that Clara learned to validate her worth and achievements, strengthening her relationship with herself.

In addition to rediscovering her artistic talents, Clara invested time in building and strengthening her friendships. She realized that these platonic relationships provided a form of emotional support and connection that was different yet equally valuable as romantic ties. Regular meetups, art collaborations, and travel with friends created a support network that was both uplifting and grounding. These friendships provided a safe space for Clara to express her vulnerabilities and celebrate her successes, contributing to a deeper sense of belonging and community. This network enhanced her emotional resilience and helped her develop communication skills and empathy, key components of secure attachment.

Personal therapy also played a crucial role in Clara's journey. Weekly sessions with a therapist skilled in attachment theory provided her with insights into her relational patterns and the underlying fears that fueled her previous anxious attachments. Therapy became a transformative tool, enabling Clara to unravel the layers of her emotions and understand the roots of her insecurities. Through cognitive-behavioral techniques, she learned to challenge her fear of abandonment and rewrite the narratives that had long governed her self-esteem. This therapeutic process was integral in building the internal security that Clara needed to navigate not only her personal life but also her interactions with others.

Clara's story is a powerful testament to the fact that securing attachment does not require a romantic partner; rather, it requires a commitment to one's growth and emotional well-being. Her journey underscores the importance of individual development in cultivating a secure attachment style. By focusing on personal passions, building strong friendships, and engaging in therapy, Clara enriched her life and prepared herself for future relationships from a position of strength and security.

As Clara's experience illustrates, the path to secure attachment often involves embracing one's singlehood as an opportunity for growth and self-reflection. This perspective shift is crucial for anyone who finds themselves single and struggling with feelings of insecurity or inadequacy. Embracing singleness as a constructive and enriching phase can lead to profound personal development and a secure sense of self that benefits all forms of relationships.

Furthermore, Clara's transition into a healthy romantic relationship later in life serves as a hopeful narrative for single readers. When she eventually chose to date again, Clara entered the relationship with a clear understanding of her worth and a solid foundation of self-love and independence. This new relationship was markedly different from her past experiences—it was characterized by mutual respect, emotional availability, and healthy communication. Clara's partner, who had also spent significant time focusing on personal growth, shared her values and commitment to maintaining a secure, supportive relationship. Together, they navigated their partnership with an awareness and maturity that fostered lasting intimacy and trust.

Clara's story, along with many others like hers, illuminates the transformative power of focusing on personal development during singleness. It challenges the conventional narrative that secure attachment is solely cultivated within romantic contexts and offers a broader, more inclusive understanding of how individuals can achieve emotional security and fulfillment. For single readers, this account provides not only inspiration but also practical guidance on leveraging singleness as a powerful phase for personal growth, emotional healing, and the development of secure attachments.

FAMILY DYNAMICS AND ATTACHMENT HEALING

The intricate web of family dynamics plays a pivotal role in shaping our attachment styles. Often, the patterns and roles we observe and adopt within our family units lay the groundwork for how we approach relationships outside this nucleus. Recognizing and reshaping these familial interactions can be a profound step toward healing from anxious attachment. This healing not only affects individual members but can ripple through the family, fostering healthier interactions and strengthening bonds.

One of the most transformative aspects of family dynamics is the role each member plays. In many families, roles can become rigid, with certain members consistently taking on the caretaker role, while others might be labeled as the "troublemaker" or the "peacemaker." These roles can significantly influence how individuals view themselves and interact with the world. For instance, a child who consistently takes on the caretaker role may develop an anxious attachment style, constantly feeling the need to care for others' emotional needs at the expense of their own. By examining and discussing these roles within a therapeutic setting, families can begin to break down these patterns, allowing members to explore and adopt new roles. This shift not only alleviates the pressure on the individual members but also encourages a more balanced and healthy way for the family to function as a unit.

Family therapy has shown profound success in facilitating this kind of transformation. Therapists work with families to uncover and understand the underlying dynamics that contribute to anxious attachment styles. By creating a safe space for open dialogue, family members can express their thoughts and feelings, which might have been suppressed or misunderstood. This process is crucial in unraveling the complex interactions that define a family's emotional landscape. For example, a family might discover that their communication style tends to minimize or dismiss expressions of vulnerability, which can contribute to feelings of insecurity and fear of abandonment in one of the members. Through therapy, they can learn new ways of communicating that validate and support each member's emotional needs.

Improving communication within the family is often a direct result of successful family therapy. As families learn to express their needs, fears, and desires more clearly and respectfully, they understand each other better and develop deeper empathy for each other's experiences. This enhanced communication leads to healthier attachment styles among family members, as they feel more secure and valued within the family unit. The positive changes in how they relate to one another often extend beyond the family, influencing their relationships with friends, colleagues, and romantic partners. The skills learned in family therapy—such as active listening, expressing emotions without judgment, and supporting each other's growth—become invaluable tools that members carry into every arena of their lives.

Perhaps the most significant impact of healing attachment issues within a family is the potential to break generational cycles of insecure attachments. As parents and children learn healthier ways of relating and supporting each other, they lay the groundwork for a new legacy of secure attachment that can transcend generations. This not only benefits the individuals directly involved but also future generations who will inherit these healthier relational patterns. The ripple effects of such healing are vast and profound, offering hope and a path toward emotional resilience and fulfillment that can last a lifetime.

In this exploration of family dynamics and attachment healing, we've seen how changes within the family structure can lead to significant emotional growth and healthier relationships. By addressing and reshaping familial roles, engaging in family therapy, and improving communication, families can overcome patterns of anxious attachment and foster a legacy of security and understanding. This chapter not only highlights the challenges faced by families but also celebrates the remarkable transformations that are possible when families come together to heal and support one another.

As we close this chapter, we carry forward the understanding that our families, with all their complexities, hold the key to unlocking patterns of fear and insecurity that may have seemed unchangeable. The journey continues as we explore further into the emotional landscapes that shape our lives, armed with the knowledge and strategies to cultivate healthier, more fulfilling relationships.

8

MAINTAINING EMOTIONAL HEALTH AND RELATIONSHIP SUCCESS

I magine a life where each day begins not with a rush of anxiety but with a sense of peace and preparedness. In this chapter, we explore the profound role of self-care in maintaining not only your emotional health but also securing your relationships. Over my extensive career in nursing, spanning more than three decades, I have witnessed firsthand how a well-tailored routine of self-care can serve as the bedrock for emotional resilience and attachment security. Here, we delve into how integrating effective self-care routines can transform your day-to-day experience, providing stability and reducing the intensity of attachment-based fears.

THE ROLE OF SELF-CARE IN ATTACHMENT SECURITY

Emphasize Routine Self-Care

The importance of routine self-care cannot be overstated, especially for those dealing with anxious attachment. Regular self-care acts as a keystone habit, influencing various aspects of your life by instilling order and calm. Think of it as tuning an instrument before a performance; self-care prepares and maintains your emotional resilience, allowing you to handle the ups and downs of relationships with greater ease. Activities such as exercise, meditation, and engaging in hobbies do not merely fill your time; they fundamentally enhance your emotional balance. Exercise, for instance, is not just about physical health but also about releasing pent-up stress, enabling you to approach your relationships with a clearer, more relaxed mindset. Similarly, meditation can help in managing anxiety and fostering a state of mindfulness, which is crucial for responding rather than reacting to relationship dynamics.

Customize Self-Care Practices

Each person's needs and lifestyles are different, and so should be their self-care practices. Customizing your self-care routine is about identifying what rejuvenates you both emotionally and physically. Begin by assessing your current lifestyle and emotional needs. Ask yourself what activities make you feel more secure and less anxious. Is it a quiet morning walk? Perhaps journaling at the end of the day? Or maybe a creative outlet like painting or writing? Once identified, integrate these activities into your daily routine in ways that feel natural and enjoyable. It's essential that these activities are not viewed as another chore but as nurturing practices that enhance your well-being.

Link Self-Care to Emotional Stability

Consistent self-care routines play a critical role in stabilizing your emotions, directly impacting your attachment security. These routines help establish predictability that can be deeply reassuring for someone with an anxious attachment style, counteracting the chaos that uncertainty and fear can bring into relationships. By engaging in regular self-care, you create a buffer against the vicissitudes of relational dynamics, equipping yourself with a steadier emotional base. This stability is crucial not only for managing personal anxiety but also for interacting with partners in a calm, assured manner that fosters trust and mutual respect.

Encourage Self-Care Plans

To integrate self-care effectively into your life, I recommend creating a comprehensive self-care plan that addresses your daily, weekly, and monthly needs. This plan should include various activities that cater to different aspects of your well-being: physical, emotional, and mental. Start by setting specific, achievable goals—for example, dedicating thirty minutes to meditation each morning or attending a dance class twice a week. Incorporate regular check-ins with yourself to assess how these activities are affecting your emotional health and adjust your plan as needed. Remember, the objective is to build a sustainable practice that supports your emotional health and nurtures your relationships consistently.

Through these detailed strategies, you can transform self-care from a sporadic luxury into a fundamental component of your daily life, anchoring your emotional health and enhancing your relational stability. As you cultivate these practices, you'll likely notice a profound shift not only in how you relate to others but also in how you perceive and engage with yourself. This chapter is a call to action to prioritize yourself, build a routine that safeguards your emotional health, and step into each day with renewed confidence and stability in your relationships.

LIFELONG STRATEGIES FOR EMOTIONAL REGULATION

Navigating the complexities of emotions requires more than just temporary fixes; it demands a deep, structured approach to truly understand and manage the feelings that surge through us daily. As someone deeply invested in nurturing emotional wellness, I've seen the transformative power of advanced emotional regulation strategies such as cognitive reframing, assertiveness training, and advanced mindfulness techniques. These tools are not just methods but pathways to a more stable and fulfilling life, especially for those grappling with anxious attachment.

Cognitive reframing is a technique that involves changing your frame of reference to view a situation from a different perspective. This is particularly valuable when dealing with the fears and insecurities characteristic of anxious attachment. For example, if you often find yourself worrying about your partner's fidelity without reason, cognitive reframing can help shift your view from one of suspicion to one of understanding and trust, considering facts over fears. This technique encourages you to challenge and alter negative thought patterns, fostering a healthier, more balanced outlook on relationships and life events.

Assertiveness training, on the other hand, equips you with the skills needed to express your thoughts and feelings openly and respectfully, without anxiety or aggression. For those who struggle with voicing their needs due to fear of abandonment, learning to communicate assertively is a game changer. It empowers you to maintain your personal boundaries and express your needs clearly, reducing misunderstandings and building stronger, more honest relationships. Through role-play and real-life application, assertiveness training helps you practice and integrate these communication skills, ensuring they become a natural part of your interactions.

Advanced mindfulness techniques, such as mindful self-compassion and focused meditation practices, offer deep dives into the emotional self, allowing you to address and soothe the anxieties at the heart of anxious attachment. These practices teach you to observe your emotions without judgment, understand their origins, and gently shift your responses to be more measured and mindful. By regularly engaging in these practices, you cultivate a stable and centered emotional state, significantly improving your capacity to handle relationship stresses and personal challenges more effectively.

Create a Personal Emotional Toolkit

To navigate the varied landscapes of our emotional worlds, it is crucial to have a well-equipped toolkit at your disposal. This toolkit should be as unique as you are, tailored to fit your specific emotional needs and lifestyle. Start by assessing the situations that typically trigger your anxiety or insecurity. Once identified, select tools from the advanced strategies discussed—like cognitive reframing for shifting perspective in stress-inducing situations or assertiveness training for moments when you need to express your boundaries more clearly.

Also include personalized coping mechanisms that you've found effective, whether it be a short walk to clear your mind, a specific breathing technique, or a go-to meditation session that helps center your thoughts. The key is to have a variety of tools, as no single method fits all scenarios. By compiling these into a personal emotional toolkit, you ensure that you are prepared to handle emotional upheavals with agility and resilience, minimizing the impact on your daily life and relationships.

Discuss the Role of Emotional Intelligence

Emotional Intelligence plays a pivotal role in how we understand and manage our emotions and those of others. It's a skill set that includes emotional awareness, the ability to apply emotions to tasks like thinking and problem-solving, and the management of emotions, which includes regulating your own emotions and cheering up or calming down other people. Improving your emotional intelligence can significantly affect your relationships, enhancing how you connect, communicate, and empathize with others and, most importantly, how you understand yourself.

To enhance your emotional intelligence, start by practicing self-awareness. This involves recognizing your emotions as they occur and understanding the impact they have on your thoughts and actions. Regular self-reflection can help you become more aware of your emotional triggers and patterns, which is the first step in learning to manage them better. Additionally, try to practice empathy by actively listening to and considering others' perspectives. This improves your relationships and provides deeper insights into human emotions, including your own.

Promote Continuous Learning

The landscape of emotional regulation is ever-evolving, and staying engaged with the latest research and methods is crucial for continual growth. I encourage you to seek out books, courses, and workshops that focus on advanced emotional regulation strategies and emotional intelligence. These resources can provide you with new tools and techniques, enhancing your ability to manage your emotions effectively.

Additionally, consider joining seminars and talks on emotional health that can offer new perspectives and insights into managing attachment-related issues. Many communities and online platforms offer sessions with experts where you can learn and even share your experiences and strategies, contributing to a broader understanding of emotional health.

Engaging in these activities enriches your knowledge and keeps you connected to a community of learners and practitioners, ensuring that your journey in emotional regulation is both supported and dynamic.

NURTURING RESILIENCE: FACING FUTURE RELATIONSHIP CHALLENGES

Resilience in the context of relationships is your ability to bounce back from setbacks and maintain a positive connection even in the face of challenges. It's a crucial element for anyone, particularly for those dealing with anxious attachment styles, as it empowers you to handle the ups and downs inherent in any relationship. Resilience is not about avoiding conflict or difficulties but about navigating through them with grace and strength, ensuring that these challenges do not derail the progress you have made in your personal growth and relationships.

Building resilience involves a combination of self-awareness, positive thinking, and adaptive coping strategies. Developing a strong sense of self is the cornerstone of this process. This means clearly under-standing your values, strengths, and limitations. When you know who you are and what you stand for, it's easier to remain steady during relationship turbulence. Engaging in regular self-reflection can help solidify this sense of self. You might consider setting aside time each week to reflect on your experiences, how you handled various situations, and what you learned about yourself in the process. This ongoing reflection helps reinforce your core values and enhances your resilience by reminding you of your capabilities and growth.

Maintaining a hopeful outlook is another vital strategy in building resilience. Hope allows you to see the possibilities in the future, even when the present seems fraught with difficulties. Cultivating opti-mism can be as simple as practicing gratitude—regularly acknowl-edging the good in your life can shift your focus from what's going wrong to what's going right. This shift doesn't mean ignoring the problems you face but provides a more balanced perspective that can motivate you to navigate challenges more effectively. Additionally, setting achievable goals for your relationship can foster hope. These goals can be as straightforward as planning a weekly date night or as significant as working toward a shared long-term vision. The key is to set clear, realistic targets that encourage both partners to work together, strengthening the bond and building resilience.

Adaptive coping skills are also essential for resilience. These are the strategies you use to manage stress and regulate your emotions. Skills such as deep breathing, mindfulness, and even physical activities like yoga can help maintain your emotional equilibrium. Developing a routine that incorporates these practices can make them more effec-tive, especially during times of stress. For instance, if you know that discussions about certain topics are likely to be stressful, you might schedule a time to practice mindfulness or go for a walk beforehand to ensure you're in a calm, centered state when you engage in these conversations.

Role-Play Scenarios

To further enhance your resilience, consider engaging in role-play scenarios that simulate potential relationship challenges. These exercises can be particularly beneficial in helping you practice and refine your responses to conflict or stress. For example, you could role-play a situation where you and your partner disagree on a significant issue like finances or family commitments. One person could present their viewpoint while the other practices responding with empathy, assertiveness, and openness. Afterward, discuss what was effective and what could be improved. These role-plays not only help you develop more effective communication and problem-solving skills but also build confidence in your ability to handle difficult situations, reinforcing your resilience.

Share Inspirational Stories

Sharing stories of resilience can also be profoundly motivating. Consider the story of Carol, a woman who faced significant challenges in her marriage due to her husband's chronic illness. Despite the stress and uncertainty brought on by his health issues, Carol remained committed to supporting her husband and strengthening their relationship. She developed a network of support, engaged in regular self-care, and learned as much as she could about his condition to manage it effectively together. Her story is a powerful example of how resilience, underpinned by love, commitment, and proactive coping strategies, can lead to deeper connections and relationship satisfaction.

Each of these strategies—developing a strong sense of self, maintaining a hopeful outlook, practicing adaptive coping skills, engaging in role-play, and drawing inspiration from others' stories—plays a crucial role in building and nurturing resilience. This resilience empowers you to face future relationship challenges with confidence, knowing that you have the tools and the strength to handle them. As you continue to cultivate these skills, you'll find that not only are your relationships stronger, but you are also more equipped to enjoy a fulfilling, emotionally healthy life.

THE IMPORTANCE OF COMMUNITY AND SUPPORT SYSTEMS

Navigating the complexities of attachment styles and personal growth is not just a solitary endeavor; it thrives in the nurturing environment of community support. A supportive community can provide a robust scaffold for your emotional health, offering not just comfort but also practical assistance and a sense of belonging that are vital for anyone, particularly those working through issues of anxious attachment. When you are part of a community, you gain access to a diverse toolkit of perspectives and experiences, enriching your own understanding and coping strategies. This communal support can manifest in various forms—emotional empathy during tough times, practical help when you're overwhelmed, and affirmation of your progress— all of which fortify your journey towards secure attachment.

Building a supportive network, however, requires intention and effort. Start by exploring groups that align with your interests and values. This could be a local book club, a yoga class, or an online forum dedicated to mental health. The key is to find spaces where you feel safe and valued, allowing you to be open and honest about your struggles and victories. Engaging in activities that resonate with your personal interests not only makes the process of building connections more enjoyable but also increases the likelihood of meeting like-minded individuals who can relate to and reinforce your emotional goals.

Active participation in these communities is crucial. It's one thing to attend meetings or join online chats, but another to engage fully. Share your experiences, listen actively to others, and offer your support. Volunteering, for example, can be a powerful way to give back to the community that supports you, strengthening your own emotional resilience as you bolster that of others. Furthermore, organizing social events or starting a support group can also enhance your leadership skills and deepen your connections within the community, creating a network that thrives on mutual support and understanding.

The role of online communities in providing support cannot be underestimated, especially for those who may not have access to in-person groups due to geographical, physical, or psychological barriers. Online platforms can offer a lifeline, connecting you with global networks of support where advice, experiences, and encouragement are shared around the clock. These virtual spaces often offer anonymity and accessibility, making it easier to share sensitive personal issues and receive support without the fear of stigma. Engaging in these communities can be as simple as joining a webinar, participating in a virtual workshop, or contributing to forum discussions. Each interaction, whether big or small, contributes to a larger tapestry of communal support that holds each member up.

Through these strategies, your understanding of community support transforms from a concept to a practical, vital resource that enhances your emotional health and bolsters your attachment security. As you weave these threads of connection, participation, and leadership into your daily life, your support network becomes a cornerstone of your journey towards healthier, more secure attachments.

TEACHING OTHERS ABOUT ATTACHMENT: SPREADING AWARENESS

One of the most empowering actions you can take in the realm of personal growth and emotional health is sharing your knowledge and experiences with others. This aids their understanding, deepens their own insights, and reinforces their commitment to healthy attachment practices. Imagine the impact you could have by guiding someone through the complexities of attachment theory or by simply sharing how these concepts have transformed your own relationships. This act of teaching becomes a ripple effect, spreading awareness and fostering healthier communities.

Encouraging you to educate others about attachment theory involves more than just recounting your experiences; it's about actively engaging in conversations that promote a more in-depth understanding of how attachment styles influence our interactions and emotional well-being. You can start these conversations casually, perhaps by sharing an insight during a coffee break with a coworker or while catching up with a friend. For instance, if a friend is struggling with relationship issues, you might introduce the concept of attachment styles to help them understand the dynamics at play. This can provide them with a new lens through which to view their relationship challenges and encourage them to explore further.

To effectively share this knowledge, it is useful to have a range of resources at your disposal. Books such as *attached* by Amir Levine and Rachel Heller offer a comprehensive overview of attachment theory and are accessible to those unfamiliar with psychological jargon. Websites like The Attachment Project provide articles, quizzes, and courses that can be easily shared with friends or family members interested in learning more about their attachment style. Additionally, scholarly articles from psychology databases can offer more in-depth information for those interested in the nuances and latest research in the field.

Incorporating lessons about attachment into everyday life can also extend to more formal settings, such as parenting or mentoring. For parents, understanding attachment theory can profoundly affect how they relate to their children, helping to foster secure attachment from an early age. Suggestions for incorporating these lessons include using empathetic communication, being consistently responsive to the child's needs, and modeling healthy emotional expressions. Mentors and coaches can integrate attachment principles in their guidance, helping mentees understand their relationship patterns and how these may be impacting their personal and professional lives. By weaving these insights into your interactions, you enhance your relationships and provide valuable tools for others to understand and improve their own.

Discussing the benefits of teaching others about attachment can further illuminate the value of this endeavor. When you teach, you reinforce your own understanding and engage in a process of reflection and synthesis that can deepen your grasp of the subject. This process often leads to new insights and a stronger commitment to applying these principles in your own life. Moreover, teaching enhances your communication skills, especially in explaining complex ideas in simple terms, which is a valuable skill in both personal and professional contexts. It also builds your confidence as you see the positive impact of your knowledge on others' lives, which in turn can motivate you to continue your learning and growth in the field of attachment and relationships.

By embracing the role of a teacher, whether in informal or formal settings, you become an advocate for emotional health and relational well-being. This role not only enriches the lives of those around you but also contributes to your own journey toward a more secure and insightful life. As you continue to share and teach, remember that each conversation, each piece of advice, and each shared resource has the potential to initiate change, inspire growth, and foster healthier, more fulfilling relationships.

REVIEW AND REFLECT: CONTINUOUSLY EVOLVING YOUR ATTACHMENT STYLE

In the evolving landscape of personal development, the significance of regularly reflecting on one's growth journey cannot be overstated. Particularly for those navigating the complexities of attachment styles, periodic self-review serves as both a compass and a map, guiding you through the terrain of emotional health and relational dynamics. This habit of reflection ensures that you remain not only responsive to your evolving needs but also proactive in cultivating deeply satisfying and nurturing relationships.

Encourage Regular Self-Review

The practice of self-review is akin to tending a garden; it is necessary to regularly check on its progress, prune away the unnecessary, and nurture the growth areas. For you, this means periodically assessing how your attachment style might be influencing your current relationships and overall emotional health. Set aside time each month to reflect on specific instances where your attachment style was evident and consider how effectively you managed your emotions and interactions. Did you feel secure and connected, or were there moments of anxiety and doubt? How did you handle these situations? This regular audit allows you to recognize patterns, celebrate progress, and identify areas needing attention, ensuring that your growth does not stagnate.

Provide Tools for Self-Assessment

To aid in this self-review process, various tools can be amazingly effective. Journals serve as a personal archive where you can document thoughts, feelings, and incidents that reflect your attachment style in action. Keeping a journal encourages a routine of daily reflection and provides a valuable record of your emotional trends over time. Checklists can also be useful, especially when dealing with complex emotions or behaviors related to attachment issues. They can help you track specific behaviors and triggers, making it easier to identify patterns and measure progress. Additionally, reflective exercises such as writing letters to your future or past self can provide more in-depth insights into your emotional journey and attachment evolution, offering perspectives that might not surface in daily journaling.

Assessment tools and crafted questionnaires specifically designed for identifying anxious attachment styles can be particularly beneficial. Websites like **AttachmentProject.com**, **PsychCentral.com**, and

TherapistAid.com offer structured assessments and self-report questionnaires that help you explore your attachment behaviors, thoughts, and feelings. These tools provide clarity on how anxious attachment manifests in your relationships. By regularly using these questionnaires, you can track changes over time, measure your progress, and identify areas that need more attention. Whether used independently or alongside other self-assessment methods, these tools provide a comprehensive approach to understanding and addressing your attachment style.

Discuss the Importance of Adaptability

Adaptability in personal growth is essential, particularly in the context of evolving attachment styles. As your life situations change —perhaps through new relationships or deeper self-understanding —so too might your approach to managing and understanding your attachment style. This adaptability isn't about inconsistency but about being responsive to your continuing growth and changing circumstances. It means being open to modifying your strategies as you gain more in-depth insights into your attachment behaviors or as your relationships evolve. For instance, techniques that helped manage your attachment anxiety in the past may become less effective as you grow, necessitating new strategies or adaptations. This flexibility ensures that your approach to personal and relational growth remains dynamic and effective, truly reflecting your developmental journey.

Create a Culture of Continuous Improvement

Fostering a mindset of lifelong learning and continuous improvement is crucial in the realm of emotional and relational health. This mindset encourages an ongoing commitment to deepening your understanding of attachment theories and expanding your interpersonal skills. Engage with new books, podcasts, and seminars that challenge and expand your knowledge. Participate in workshops and discussion groups that explore themes of emotional health and relational dynamics. Each of these activities broadens your perspective and reinforces your commitment to growth and learning, keeping you engaged and proactive in your personal development journey.

In this chapter, we've explored how regular self-review and adaptability play crucial roles in the ongoing process of understanding and evolving your attachment style. By incorporating self-assessment tools and fostering a culture of continuous improvement, you equip yourself with the means to navigate the complexities of relationships with greater awareness and efficacy. As you reflect on your growth and adapt your strategies, you enhance your emotional and relational health and move closer to the life of connection and security you aspire to.

As we close this chapter, remember that the path to secure attachment and emotional wellness is both rewarding and demanding. It requires persistence, courage, and, most importantly, a willingness to embrace change and growth continuously. Carry forward the insights and strategies from this chapter as you continue to cultivate a life rich in healthy relationships and personal fulfillment.

YOUR VOICE MATTERS: SHARE YOUR EXPERIENCE

Help Others on Their Journey

"The greatest gift you can give someone is the wisdom of your experience."
anonymous

Congratulations on completing the *Anxious Attachment Recovery Solution!* Your journey to understanding and healing is remarkable, and I hope this book has been a valuable guide for you.

Now, I'd like to ask for your help. Your insights and thoughts could be the guiding light for someone just beginning their journey. Sharing your experience could inspire, encourage, and support others seeking to overcome their fears and build secure, lasting relationships.

Leaving a review is simple and takes just a minute, but it has a powerful impact. Your review could...

- ...help someone struggling with anxious attachment find the courage to start their healing process.
- ...guide a reader to the tools they need to boost their self-esteem and emotional stability.
- ...encourage others to connect with their inner child and overcome past traumas.
- ...support someone in their quest to build secure and fulfilling relationships.

By sharing your experience, you're not just reviewing a book—you're contributing to a community of people committed to growth and healing.

To leave your review, simply scan the QR code below:

Thank you with heartfelt gratitude, Luzivette Martinez, RN

CONCLUSION

As we draw this guide to a close, let's take a moment to reflect on the significant journey you've embarked upon. From the initial understanding of anxious attachment and its deep-rooted origins in your early experiences to the empowering steps towards cultivating secure attachment patterns, this book has been a roadmap through the complex terrains of emotional landscapes and relationships. Together, we've navigated the signs of anxious attachment, delved into the transformative process of connecting with your inner child, and explored practical strategies for building emotional resilience and secure connections.

We've covered vital ground here, from understanding the psychological frameworks that underpin attachment styles to engaging in hands-on exercises designed to foster self-awareness, emotional regulation, and, ultimately, secure relationships. The key takeaways from our journey emphasize that healing from anxious attachment is not only possible but is a transformative process that can significantly enhance your quality of life. Secure attachments bring peace, stability, and joy into relationships that once may have been battlegrounds of fear and uncertainty.

However, remember, the conclusion of this book is not the end of your journey. It is, instead, a stepping stone towards ongoing growth and self-discovery in your emotional and relational life. I encourage you to keep this book close as a continual reference as you apply the strategies and exercises we've discussed. Regularly reflect on your progress, and do not hesitate to revisit chapters as you encounter new challenges or achieve new insights.

I urge you to integrate the practices learned into your daily life consistently. Whether it's engaging in mindfulness exercises, practicing assertive communication, or journaling your thoughts and feelings, each step you take is a move towards a more secure and joyful future. Remember, the path of personal growth is not meant to be walked alone. Seek support when needed, whether through community resources, professional therapy, or supportive groups.

Thank you sincerely for your commitment to your healing journey. It takes courage to confront and work through the complexities of attachment issues, and your perseverance is commendable. As you move forward, carry with you not just the knowledge and strategies from this book but also a profound sense of hope and confidence in your ability to forge lasting, fulfilling relationships. Remember, the steps you've learned here are powerful tools in your ongoing quest for emotional freedom and security.

You are equipped, empowered, and on your way to transforming your relational world. Keep moving forward with optimism and the belief that the relationships you desire and deserve are within your reach. Here's to your continued journey of growth, healing, and deep, meaningful connections.

REFERENCES

1. Advances in research on attachment-related processes in adolescence and adulthood: Implications for risk and resilience. (2020). *National Center for Biotechnology Information*. https://www.ncbi.nlm. nih.gov/pmc/articles/PMC7451314/

2. Adult attachment, stress, and romantic relationships. (2016). *National Center for Biotechnology Information*. https://www.ncbi.nlm. nih.gov/pmc/articles/PMC4845754/

3. Anxious vs. avoidant attachment. (n.d.). *Simply Psychology*. Retrieved from https://www.simplypsychology.org/anxious-vs-avoidant-attachment.html

4. Attachment theory: Bowlby and Ainsworth's theory explained. (n.d.). *Verywell Mind*. Retrieved from https://www.verywellmind.com/ what-is-attachment-theory-2795337

5. Caring for your mental health. (n.d.). *National Institute of Mental Health*. Retrieved from https://www.nimh.nih.gov/health/topics/ caring-for-your-mental-health

6. Childhood trauma and adult interpersonal relationship outcomes: A systematic review and meta-analysis. (2015). *National Center for Biotechnology Information.* https://www.ncbi.nlm.nih.gov/pmc/articles/PMC4304140/

7. Conflict resolution skills. (n.d.). *HelpGuide.org.* Retrieved from https://www.helpguide.org/articles/relationships-communication/conflict-resolution-skills.htm

8. Facing my fear: How I overcame my terror of abandonment and fell in love. (2016, May 20). *The Guardian.* Retrieved from https://www.theguardian.com/commentisfree/2016/may/20/facing-my-fear-overcame-abandomnent-issues-fell-in-love

9. Evidence-based parenting interventions to promote secure attachment. (2016). *National Center for Biotechnology Information.* https://www.ncbi.nlm.nih.gov/pmc/articles/PMC4995667/

10. Healing your anxious attachment style: 7 books to read. (2023, September 18). *Crackliffe.* Retrieved from https://www.crackliffe.com/words/2023/09/18/books-to-heal-anxious-attachment

11. How to heal an anxious attachment style, according to a therapist. (n.d.). *Verywell Mind.* Retrieved from https://www.verywellmind.com/how-to-heal-an-anxious-attachment-style-8643714

12. How to move from anxious attachment to secure. (n.d.). *Simply Psychology.* Retrieved from https://www.simplypsychology.org/how-to-move-from-anxious-attachment-to-secure.html

13. How to use mindfulness therapy for anxiety: 15 exercises. (n.d.). *Positive Psychology.* Retrieved from https://positivepsychology.com/mindfulness-for-anxiety/

14. Influence of family of origin and adult romantic partners on attachment style. (2009). *National Center for Biotechnology Information.* https://www.ncbi.nlm.nih.gov/pmc/articles/PMC2689376/

15. Inner child healing: 35 practical tools for growing beyond your childhood wounds. (n.d.). *Positive Psychology.* Retrieved from https://positivepsychology.com/inner-child-healing/

16. 11 tips for a morning routine that supports mental health. (n.d.). *Good Therapy.* Retrieved from https://www.goodtherapy.org/blog/11-tips-for-a-morning-routine-that-supports-mental-health-1022197/

17. 50 journal prompts for anxious attachment that'll ease you. (n.d.). *WeMindGrowth.* Retrieved from https://wemindgrowth.com/journal-prompts-for-anxious-attachment/

18. 10 best mental health and therapy apps of 2024. (2024). *Verywell Mind.* Retrieved from https://www.verywellmind.com/best-mental-health-apps-4692902

19. Self-silencing: The mental health impact. (n.d.). *Newport Institute.* Retrieved from https://www.newportinstitute.com/resources/empowering-young-adults/self-silencing/

20. Secure attachment: Signs, benefits, and how to cultivate it. (n.d.). *Verywell Mind.* Retrieved from https://www.verywellmind.com/secure-attachment-signs-benefits-and-how-to-cultivate-it-8628802

21. Shifting attachment style through group therapy. (n.d.). *Holistic Psychotherapy Boulder.* Retrieved from https://www.holisticpsychotherapyboulder.com/blog/shifting-attachment-style-through-group-therapy

22. Social support mediates the association between attachment style and well-being. (2022). *National Center for Biotechnology Information*. https://www.ncbi.nlm.nih.gov/pmc/articles/PMC9027231/

23. Stafford, A. (n.d.). Active listening: The key to building stronger relationships. Retrieved from https://allenstafford.com/active-listening-the-key-to-building-stronger-relationships/

24. Strengths-based therapy: Definition and techniques. (n.d.). *Verywell Mind*. Retrieved from https://www.verywellmind.com/strengths-based-therapy-definition-and-techniques-5211679

25. The importance of empathy in relationships. (n.d.). *Array Behavioral Care*. Retrieved from https://arraybc.com/the-importance-of-empathy-in-relationships

26. The impact of childhood trauma on adult functioning. (2023, April). *Psychology Today*. Retrieved from https://www.psychologytoday.com/us/blog/understanding-ptsd/202304/the-impact-of-childhood-trauma-on-adult-functioning

27. Understanding fear of abandonment. (n.d.). *Verywell Mind*. Retrieved from https://www.verywellmind.com/fear-of-abandonment-2671741

28. 5 advanced techniques for emotional self-control. (n.d.). *Medium*. Retrieved from https://medium.com/@isasworldlc/5-advanced-techniques-for-emotional-self-control-cfe1c5c4915c

29. 7 ways to make a relationship more resilient. (2023, October). *Psychology Today*. Retrieved from https://www.psychologytoday.com/us/blog/the-psychology-of-relationships/202310/7-ways-to-make-your-relationship-more-resilient

www.ingramcontent.com/pod-product-compliance
Lightning Source LLC
Chambersburg PA
CBHW020410130626
46549CB00006B/2500

* 9 7 9 8 9 9 1 9 9 2 6 1 9 *